بِسْمِ اللهِ الرَّحْمَنِ الرَّحِيمِ

THE ELITE STAND IN HONOUR OF THE CHOSEN ONE ﷺ

IQĀMAT AL-QIYĀMAH ʿALĀ TĀʾIN AL-QIYĀM LI-NABĪYY TIHĀMAH ﷺ

(1299 AH/1881 CE)

BY SHAYKH AL-ISLĀM
IMĀM AHMAD RIDĀ KHĀN AL-QĀDIRĪ ﵁

Translated & Annotated by
Muhammad Husain al-Qādirī

Translation of *Iqāmat Al-Qiyāmah 'Alā Tā'in Al-Qiyām Li-Nabīyy Al-Tihāmah* by Muhammad Husain al-Qādirī

Manuscript Editor: Maryam Qadri
Associate Editor: Maqsud Yusuf

Published by:

Al-Mukhtār Books, US   &   Maktab-e-Qadriah, UK
PO Box 219 | Martinsville   29/30 Walnut St | Bolton
62442   BL1 8LN
info@almukhtarbooks.com   0044 1204 529740

Library of Congress Control Number: 2011913694
ISBN: 978-0-9831488-2-1

Please visit www.almukhtarbooks.com for more titles by and about the great Reviver of Islam, Imām Ahmad Ridā Khān al-Qādirī ﷺ.

Contents

"The celebration of the *Mawlid* entails gathering with the people, reading a portion of the Qur'ān, citing the narrations about the prophetic precursors to the Prophet's mission and the wondrous signs that took place during his birth, and then eating a bit of food and leaving. As I see it, this practice is a good innovation that merits reward. That is because it is an exaltation of the Prophet's rank ﷺ and a display of delight and happiness with his noble birth."

— Imām Jalāluddīn Suyūtī ﷺ

Publisher's Notes

The book before you is of paramount importance. It was written at a time when the celebration of the Prophet's birth 鸞 was being called into question by misguided innovators (1299 AH/1881 CE). More than a century later, this book continues to answer those groups that violently oppose this meritorious practice of the People of the Prophetic Way and the Majority of Scholars (*Ahl al-Sunnah wa al-Jamā'ah*). Consequentially, it is essential reading for contemporary Muslims as it defends the practice of standing (*Qiyām*) during the celebration of the Prophet's birth 鸞 (*Mawlid*).

Iqāmat Al-Qiyāmah 'Alā Tā'in Al-Qiyām Li-Nabīyy Al-Tihāmah 鸞 is an Arabic title that means, 'A Raging Apocalypse upon he who Censures Standing in Honour of the Noble Prophet of Tihāmah 鸞'. It serves to remind, give glad tidings and warn. For the believers it reminds them about the proximity of the Day of Judgment (*Qiyāmah*) and the importance of loving and honouring the Prophet 鸞. For the detractors it warns them about the severity of their offense, and the self inflicted punishment that awaits them in this life and the next. One of the Signs of the Last Days is that people (who profess to be Muslims) will attack Allāh's Beloved Messenger 鸞 by subversively demeaning his station and honour, thus they censure standing and *Mawlid*. Imām Ahmad Ridā Khān's title 鸞 also points to this sign.

Every book authored by Imām Ahmad Ridā Khān 鸞 has a numerical value that adds up to the Hijri date in which it was written, e.g. 1299 AH. This is one of the unique hallmarks of his writing style, and testifies to his greatness in the science of numerology (*Abjad*). The reader will also notice that the author combined his mathematical genius with memorable wordplay by making *Iqāmat Al-Qiyāmah*, which appears at the beginning of the title, rhyme with its ending, *Li-Nabīyy Al-Tihāmah* ☙.

We have given preference to the English title *The Elite Stand in Honour of the Chosen One* ☙, since it encapsulates the book's thesis and refers to one of the many proofs for standing (*Qiyām*), namely, the ode of Imām as-Sarsarī ☙, which contains verses such as:

Too slight for the praise of the Chosen One is gold calligraphy,
Written on a silver page with the finest script,
And the elite stand when they hear of him;
Standing in rows or crawling on their knees

The author of *Iqāmat Al-Qiyāmah* quotes this poem because Imām Taqi al-Millati wad-Dīn as-Subkī (d. 756/1355) ☙, the celebrated Mujtahid[1] and Hadīth Master (*Hafidh*)[2], stood in reverence upon hearing this canto. Imām Ahmad Ridā Khān ☙ also drew from its fragrant nectar and wrote a brilliant pentastitch amplification (*Takhmīs*).

The folk with true praise stand
Followed by a folk who stand in ecstasy
Faces are humbled despite the hater
And the elite stand when they hear of him;
Standing in rows or crawling on their knees[3]

---

[1] *Mujtahid*: One who practices *ijtihad* or personal effort of qualified legal reasoning.
[2] *Hafidh*: One whose knowledge encompasses at least 100,000 Ahādīth in both their texts and chains of transmission.
[3] Al-Mukhtār Books and Maktab-e-Qadriah wish to thank Ihsanica Media for giving us permission to quote the poetic verses translated in *A Just Word: The Life & Legacy of Imām Ahmad Ridā Khān* [Insāf al-Imām] by Shaykh Khālid Thābit.

Iqāmat Al-Qiyāmah was written in Urdu and presumes some knowledge of the language and the historical events of that particular place (British India) and time (the 19th century). As a result, certain additions were necessary to help English-speaking Muslims living in the West understand what would have been common knowledge to the author's original audience, South Asian Muslims. However, these slight modifications do not contradict the original meaning and have been noted in brackets.

We have also applied the following honorifics using Arabic calligraphy and lettering:

    ⁂   *sall-Allāhu 'alayhi wa sallam* (Allāh's blessings and greetings of peace be upon him) following the name of our Master, Prophet Muhammad ⁂.

    ⁂   *'alayhi as-salām* (peace be upon him) following the names of other Prophets ⁂, Angels ⁂, and Khidr ⁂.

    ⁂   *'alayhā as-salām* (peace be upon her) following the name of Maryam, Mother of Jesus ⁂.

    ⁂   *radī-Allāhu 'anh/'anha* (may Allāh be pleased with him/her) following the name of a male or female Companion or Successor of the Prophet ⁂, and the venerable scholar-saints of our grand Tradition.

Before concluding, it is worth noting that Imām Ahmad Ridā Khān ⁂ was a prodigious representative of a very advanced intellectual training, an educational form that hardly has any counterpart in the modern world, be it at an undergraduate or even a graduate level. Accordingly, this *tour de force* was written when he was only twenty-seven years old after he had performed the pilgrimage (*Hajj*) to Makkah the Ennobled in 1878.[4] Here he received recognition and training from top-ranking scholars (*'Ulamā*) such as the Mufti of the Hanafī school, Shaykh Abdur Rahmān Sirāj ☙; the Shāfi'ī Imām, Shaykh Husain Salih ☙; and the Mufti of the Shāfi'ī school, Shaykh Ahmad ibn Zayn Dahlan ☙ (*Qādī al-Qudāt* [5], Makkah). He refers to the legal edicts of the Haramayn[6] scholars quite frequently in Chapter Two: What the Muslims Deem Good. Insha'Allāh, the reader will grow to appreciate this fact as he sees the depth and breadth of the author's knowledge unfold before his own eyes.

---

[4] 1296 AH
[5] *Qādī al-Qudāt*: Chief Judge.
[6] *Haramayn*: the Makkan and Madinan Sanctuaries.

Dedication

I dedicate this book to the one, who instilled the love Allāh and His Beloved Prophet ﷺ in the hearts of many, whose life was engrossed in the remembrance of Allāh and His Beloved Prophet ﷺ, our Master, the Chieftain of the Saints, *Sultan al-Awliyā, al-Ghawth al-A'ẓam Sayyidunā ash-Shaykh Muhyid'dīn 'Abd al-Qādir al-Jīlānī al-Baghdādī al-Hasanī al-Husaynī* ﷺ.

Acknowledgements

All praise is due to Allāh, the Lord of all the Worlds, and may peace and blessings be upon the Beloved Prophet, upon his Companions and all of his followers till the Day of Judgement.

This book has thus been compiled to illustrate the permissibility of standing up (*Qiyām*) out of respect for the Beloved Prophet of Allāh ﷺ. It was originally written in Urdu by the great Reviver (*Mujaddid*) of his time, Imām Ahmad Ridā Khān ؓ, who spent his entire life defending Islām and its pristine teachings through the power of his tongue and pen.

I would like to express my sincere gratitude to Mawlānā Muhammad Khalid who set aside time in order to proofread this book and Brother Hafiz Maqsud for composing and setting the book.

I would also feel a sense of ingratitude if I did not mention sister Maryam Qadri of al-Mukhtār Books (USA), who spent tireless effort proofreading the entire document with utmost care, accuracy, and precision; alongside this, she added useful comments and notes wherever needed. May Allāh the Exalted reward her and her family abundantly in both worlds, Āmīn.

Despite the most rigorous attention to detail, errors and mistakes are almost inevitable in translating such a profound work. As such, readers are encouraged to forgive any oversights on our part and bring these to our attention, thus helping us avoid such lapses in future editions.

Acknowledgements

O Allāh, the All-Merciful One! Accept our deeds and give us sincerity in our actions. O Ever-Gracious One! Send Your sublime salutations on Your Beloved Prophet and upon his Family, Descendants and Companions.

Muhammad Husain al-Qādirī
23rd Jumādā al-Ākhirah 1432 AH
1st May 2011

Author's Prologue

[The present work begins with the following question put forth to the author (Imām Ahmad Ridā Khān ﷺ) by a certain person. The resultant response from the author took the form of a comprehensive legal edict (*Fatwā*), and is presented in this book.]

QUESTION

What do the eminent scholars have to say about the issue of standing up (*Qiyām*) at the time of remembering the blessed birth of the Prophet ﷺ (*Mawlid*)? Some argue that it is forbidden and the reason they present is that it was never proven nor practiced in the first three centuries of Islām.

They also demand proofs for its validity from the sayings and practices of the blessed Companions and their Successors (*Tabi'īn*). What is the answer to their claims and demands? Please answer and be rewarded immensely.

Was-Salām,

Riyāsat Mustafā Ābād Rāmpūr (1299 AH/1881 CE)

ANSWER

All praise be to Allāh by whose command the skies have been held aloft, and blessings and salutations upon the one by whose light the pillars of the Sacred Law (*Shari'ah*) are established - he is our Master, the Beloved Prophet of Allāh ﷺ, for whom the Angels stood up in respect at the time of his birth. Blessings and

4

salutations upon his Family and Companions who always stood up to greet him; thereby, honouring him with utmost respect.

I bear witness that there in none worthy of worship besides Allāh, the Almighty. He is Alone and has no partners. And I bear witness that Muhammad ﷺ is His Servant and Prophet, who is the leader of all the Prophets.

May blessings and salutations be upon him and all the Prophets as long as the trees glorify Allāh and as long as the heavenly stars are in prostration to the Ever-Living (*Hayy*), Ever-Lasting (*Qayyūm*) Lord of all the Worlds, Āmīn.

Standing very humbly and sincerely in the presence of the owner of the Station of Praise (*Maqām al-Mahmūd*) and intercession (*Shafā'at*) ﷺ; I, the Servant of the Chosen One (`Abd al-Mustafā*), Imām Ahmad Ridā Khān ﷺ [may Allāh forgive him and grant him a place among the Pious Predecessors, Āmīn], say:

O Allāh give us guidance that is true and correct, Āmīn.

TWO VERY IMPORTANT ISSUES

There are two very important issues under discussion in this book: First, we shall ascertain the ruling on standing (*Qiyām*) and *Mawlid* from the [authentic] books and legal edicts (*Fatāwā*) of our great jurists and scholars (may Allāh elevate their ranks) by which the truth can be established and falsehood can be admonished. Second, we will answer our opponent's argument that, "this deed (of standing up for the Prophet ﷺ) did not exist in the first three centuries of Islām, thus it is an innovation and misguidance. If there was any virtue in this deed then the Companions and the

Successors would have done it." Their criticism will be answered by using their own evidence and logic.

This is the extent of their efforts by which they have branded the great and prominent leaders of the Sacred Law (*Shari'ah*) and the Sufi path (*Tariqah*) as misguided innovators, and they have no fear of Allāh nor of the Day of Reckoning, Allāh forbid!

Although scholarly verdicts (*Fatāwā*) are not open to debate, in this case it would be irrational to ignore the opponent's criticism of our view (in favor of *Qiyām*). Thus, I will present a few important points throughout my discussion of the second issue that might delight you.

Upon the the Mercy of Allāh do we rely in every step and upon Him do we depend and to Him do we turn for Help. All praise be to Allāh, Lord of all the Worlds.

Chapter One: The Chain of Authority

Allāh Almighty has sent down the most evident, luminous (*Garrā*), pure (*Baydā*), complete (*Tāmmah*), broad (*'Āmmah*), comprehensive (*Shāmilah*) and inclusive Religion. And by His grace He has made it a 'Complete Religion' and through the Mercy of His Beloved ﷺ, He has completed His favour upon us all. Allāh Almighty says,

حُرِّمَتْ عَلَيْكُمُ ٱلْمَيْتَةُ وَٱلدَّمُ وَلَحْمُ ٱلْخِنزِيرِ وَمَآ أُهِلَّ لِغَيْرِ ٱللَّهِ بِهِۦ وَٱلْمُنْخَنِقَةُ وَٱلْمَوْقُوذَةُ وَٱلْمُتَرَدِّيَةُ وَٱلنَّطِيحَةُ وَمَآ أَكَلَ ٱلسَّبُعُ إِلَّا مَا ذَكَّيْتُمْ وَمَا ذُبِحَ عَلَى ٱلنُّصُبِ وَأَن تَسْتَقْسِمُواْ بِٱلْأَزْلَٰمِ ذَٰلِكُمْ فِسْقٌ ٱلْيَوْمَ يَئِسَ ٱلَّذِينَ كَفَرُواْ مِن دِينِكُمْ فَلَا تَخْشَوْهُمْ وَٱخْشَوْنِ ٱلْيَوْمَ أَكْمَلْتُ لَكُمْ دِينَكُمْ وَأَتْمَمْتُ عَلَيْكُمْ نِعْمَتِى وَرَضِيتُ لَكُمُ ٱلْإِسْلَٰمَ دِينًا فَمَنِ ٱضْطُرَّ فِى مَخْمَصَةٍ غَيْرَ مُتَجَانِفٍ لِّإِثْمٍ فَإِنَّ ٱللَّهَ غَفُورٌ رَّحِيمٌ ۝

"This day I have perfected your religion for you and completed My favour upon you, and have chosen for you Islām as your religion" (5:3).

All praise is for Allāh who is the Lord of all the Worlds. And salutations upon him ﷺ by whose grace Allāh has bestowed upon us the bounty of the Religion and all worldly favours. And through him, Allāh will bestow upon us the bounties of the Hereafter, Allāh Willing.

All praise is for Allāh! It must be known that none of their rulings are truly based on the Holy Qur'ān. Amīr al-Mu'minīn Sayyidunā

7

'Umar ﷺ once said, "The Holy Qur'ān is enough for us."[7] However, the common folk cannot establish rulings from the verses of the Holy Qur'ān.[8] This is because the Holy Qur'ān has given us two very important rules. The first rule states:

مَّآ أَفَآءَ ٱللَّهُ عَلَىٰ رَسُولِهِۦ مِنْ أَهْلِ ٱلْقُرَىٰ فَلِلَّهِ وَلِلرَّسُولِ وَلِذِى ٱلْقُرْبَىٰ وَٱلْيَتَـٰمَىٰ وَٱلْمَسَـٰكِينِ وَٱبْنِ ٱلسَّبِيلِ كَىْ لَا يَكُونَ دُولَةًۢ بَيْنَ ٱلْأَغْنِيَآءِ مِنكُمْ ۚ وَمَآ ءَاتَىٰكُمُ ٱلرَّسُولُ فَخُذُوهُ وَمَا نَهَىٰكُمْ عَنْهُ فَٱنتَهُواْ ۚ وَٱتَّقُواْ ٱللَّهَ ۖ إِنَّ ٱللَّهَ شَدِيدُ ٱلْعِقَابِ ۝

"And whatsoever the Messenger gives you take it, and whatsoever he forbids you, abstain from that" (59:7).

I say: the verb is imperative and an imperative verb means compulsion. So the first part of this verse illustrated the obligations (*Wājibāt*) of the *Shari'ah* and the second part is negation, and negation demands prohibition thus this second type illustrates the prohibitions (*Mamnu'āt*) of the *Shari'ah*. So even though there is a description of everything in the Qur'ān, for example,

وَيَوْمَ نَبْعَثُ فِى كُلِّ أُمَّةٍ شَهِيدًا عَلَيْهِم مِّنْ أَنفُسِهِمْ ۖ وَجِئْنَا بِكَ شَهِيدًا عَلَىٰ هَـٰٓؤُلَآءِ ۚ وَنَزَّلْنَا عَلَيْكَ ٱلْكِتَـٰبَ تِبْيَـٰنًا لِّكُلِّ شَىْءٍ وَهُدًى وَرَحْمَةً وَبُشْرَىٰ لِلْمُسْلِمِينَ ۝

"And We have sent down this Qur'ān on you in which everything is clearly explained…"(16:89).

Yet no one can understand it without the teachings of the Prophet ﷺ.

---

[7] *Sahīh al-Bukhārī*, the book of `Ilm, the chapter Kitābat al-'Ilm, Qadimi Kutub Khana, Karachi, v.1, p. 22.

[8] The Holy Qur'ān is the leader (*Imām*) of Hadīth, Hadīth is the leader (*Imām*) of the Mujtahid, the Mujtahid is the leader (*Imām*) of the scholars and scholars are the leaders (*Imāms*) of the Muslims. To break this chain is misguidance.

بِٱلْبَيِّنَـٰتِ وَٱلزُّبُرِ ۗ وَأَنزَلْنَآ إِلَيْكَ ٱلذِّكْرَ لِتُبَيِّنَ لِلنَّاسِ مَا نُزِّلَ إِلَيْهِمْ وَلَعَلَّهُمْ يَتَفَكَّرُونَ ۝

"And O Beloved! We sent down to you the Remembrance that you may explain to people what was sent down to them" (16:44).

In other words, "O Beloved! The Holy Qur'ān has made everything clear for you thus inform your followers that which they need to know." Therefore, the first verse "Sent down on *you*" is specifically for the Prophet and the second verse "What was sent down to *them*" is for his followers. The second rule states:

وَمَآ أَرْسَلْنَا مِن قَبْلِكَ إِلَّا رِجَالًا نُّوحِىٓ إِلَيْهِمْ ۚ فَسْـَٔلُوٓا أَهْلَ ٱلذِّكْرِ إِن كُنتُمْ لَا تَعْلَمُونَ ۝

"O people! Ask the men of knowledge if you know not" (16:43).[9]

The new issues and problems that crop up are unlimited and if every specific legal ruling and injunction (*Juz`iyyah*) from the Ahādīth was to be named, it would still be difficult to collate them together. Moreover, how would the great *Mujtahidīn*[10] attain their

---

[9] Imām Ahmad Riḍā Khān ﷺ wrote a commentary on the book *Ma`ālim al-Tanzīl*, and under this verse (66:43), he said: "I say, this verse is from the virtues of the Qur'ān. It has ordained the people to ask scholars who possess knowledge of the Qur'ān. The scholars are guided to understand the Qur'ān through the teachings of the Beloved Prophet ﷺ. They do not rely upon their own ingenuity. Thus Allāh turned the people towards the scholars, the scholars towards Hadīth and Hadīth towards the Holy Qur'ān and indeed towards the Lord does it end. So as the Mujtahidīn may get misguided if they leave the Hadīth and turn directly to the Holy Qur'ān, similarly the non-Mujtahid will be misguided if he leaves the Mujtahidīn by turning towards the Hadīth on his own. It is for this reason that Imām Sufiyān ibn `Uyayna ﷺ, who was one of the Imāms of Hadīth at the time of Imām al-A`ẓam Abū Hanīfa ﷺ and Imām Mālik ﷺ, said, 'Hadīth is a pitfall except for the jurists [*fuqahā*].' This has been noted by Imām Ibn Hajar al-Makkī ﷺ in *Madkhal*" (Ref. See the author's notes on *Ma`ālim al-Tanzīl* under the verse 16:43-44).

[10] *Mujtahidīn*: those who practice *ijtihad* or personal effort of qualified legal reasoning.

high ranks and rewards, and how would the Community gain blessings through the difference of opinion (*Ikhtilāf al-Ummah*)?

Therefore, specific legal rulings and injunctions (*Juz'iyyāt*) in the Ahādīth have aided in deriving rulings for these new issues and problems. The explanation, of which has been made by the great *Mujtahidīn*. Despite this, the meaning of concise and difficult words still needed to be explained, which was undertaken by the upcoming scholars from one generation to another. And these clarifications and explanations go back to their origin (i.e. the Holy Qur'ān and the Hadīth). This will be the situation *"until the command of Allāh comes."*

It is in *al-Dur al-Mukhtār*, "The existence of such scholars, who have the capability to distinguish by certainty, and not merely by assumption, will always exist. And it is obligatory upon those who are not capable to turn to those who possess the capability."[11]

THERE SHALL ALWAYS BE A GROUP ON THE TRUTH

It is in *Rad al-Muhtār*, "The author has stated this positively taking it from the Hadīth of *al-Bukhārī* in which the Prophet ﷺ has said, 'There shall always remain a group in my Community who are manifest on the truth, unaffected by those who oppose them, until the command of Allāh comes.' The author's saying 'obligatory upon those who are not capable of distinction...' has been associated with the command of the Holy Qur'ān, 'Ask the men of knowledge if you know not.'"[12]

---

[11] *Al-Dur al-Mukhtār*, introduction of the book, Mujtaba'i press, Delhi, vol.1, p. 15.
[12] *Rad al-Muhtār*, introduction of the book, Dar Ihya Turath al-'Arabi, Beirut, vol.1, p. 53.

The great Gnostic, Sayyidī ʿAbdul Wahhāb Shaʿrāni ⬥, writes in his book, *Mizān al-Shariat al-Kubrā*, "If a scholar explains the words of a previous scholar then it is due to some insight, which he has been given from the Prophet ⬥. Therefore, in reality, the grace of the Prophet ⬥ is on all of his Community (*Ummah*). This is because the Prophet has given them this insight of explaining words which were concise. Similarly, the grace of the scholars is upon those who come after them, because if someone went around those who came before them and went to those above them, then he has broken the chain of transmission to the Prophet ⬥, thus not enabling him to explain concise and difficult words.

My brothers, think! If the Prophet ⬥ was not to explain the concise words of the Qurʾān then they would have remained difficult for us to understand. Similarly, if the *Mujtahidīn* did not explain the difficult terms of the Ahādīth then they would have remained difficult for us to understand to this very day. Thus if this reality was not to be handed down from one generation to the next, then no commentary, explanation, nor any annotation would have been written, nor would the scholars have written commentaries upon (previous) commentaries.[13]

The reader can bear witness to this that initially the 'Manifest' books (*Dhāhir al-Riwāyah*)[14] and then the 'Rare' books (*Nawādir*)[15]

---

[13] *Mizān al-Shariat al-Kubrā*, Fasl Mimmā Yadluku ʿAlā Sihhati Irtibātu Jamīʿ Aqwām ʿUlamāi al-Shariah, Mustafa Al-Babi, Egypt, vol.1, p. 37.

[14] *Dhāhir al-Riwāyah*: are those legal rulings which are mentioned in the six books of Imām Muhammad ⬥ (student of Imām al-Aʿẓam Abū Hanīfa ⬥). The six books are *al-Mabsūt, al-Ziyādāt, al-Jāmiʿ al-Sagīr, Al-Siyar al-Sagīr, al-Jāmiʿ al-Kabīr* and *al-Siyar al-Kabīr*. These are known as *Dhāhir al-Riwāyah* because these rulings are mass-transmitted (*Tawatur*) and well-known.

[15] *Nawādir al-Riwāyah* are all books narrated by our Imāms which have been reported in books besides the six mentioned above. Like, *al-Haruniyyāt, al-*

were written. Then the books of 'Indigenous Literary Genre' (*Nawāzil*) and 'Narratives' (*Wāqi'āt*) were written. Thereafter, the 'Short Texts' (*Mutūn*), the 'Commentaries' (*Shurūh*), the 'Marginal Notes' (*Hawāshih*) and 'Legal Verdicts' (*Fatāwā*) from time to time were written, and in every age, the new generation of scholars kept adding to the previous works and these new works were widely accepted. All these works explain the concise meanings of the Holy Qur'ān and the Hadīth.

Nisāb al-Ihtisāb and *Fatāwā 'Ālamgirī* were written in the seventeenth century during the reign of Sultān 'Ālamgīr (d. 1118 AH/1707 CE). Some of the specific legal inductions (*Juziyyāt*) in these books **cannot** be found in the previous books, because the issues facing the Community at that time were different from those of their predecessors. Moreover, the subjects discussed in the books of 'Indigenous Literary Genre' (*Nawāzil*) and 'Narratives' (*Wāqi'āt*)[16] **do not** address contemporary issues. Now if someone asked us for evidence regarding this matter demanding proofs from the time of the Companions and the Successors (*Tābi'in*), or specifically asked for evidence from the works of Imām Abū Hanīfa ﷺ and his two closest students ﷺ (*Sāhibayn*), then surely we would have no choice but to consider this individual misguided or insane. And after *Fatāwā 'Ālamgirī* there were books written which Hanafi scholars depend on, such as *Fatāwā As'adiyya, Fatāwā Hāmidiyya, Tahtāwi 'Alā Marāqi al-Falāh, 'Uqūd al-Duriyya, Rad al-Muhtār* and *Rasā'il Shāmi;* besides the first two, the rest were written in the thirteenth century. The detractors of *Qiyām* use them as references, but you will find

---

Kisaniyāt, al-Jurjāniyāt al-Ruqiyyāt by Imām Muhammad, *al-Mujarrad* by Imam Hasan ibn Ziyād ﷺ and *al-Amalī* by Imām Abū Yusuf ﷺ.

[16] *Nawāzil* and *Waqi'āt* are those rulings derived by the jurists (*Fuqahā*) at the time they were posed the questions. They used the rulings laid down by Imām Abū Hanīfa and his students to derive the answers to the questions (see the preface of *Rad al-Muhtār,* the levels of scholars, vol.1, p.225).

issues in these books that were not present in the time of the Pious Predecessors (*Salaf al-Salih*). The detractors not only use the *Fatāwā* of Shāh 'Abd al-'Azīz ad-Dehlawī (d. 1239 AH/1823 CE) 鐵, but they also depend on *Mi'at Masā'il Wa Arba`īn*. I wonder if they can show me a single legal induction (*Juz`iyyah*) from these books that goes back to the time of the Companions, the Successors (*Tabi'īn*), or even '*Ālamgirī* and *Rad al-Muhtār*?

Subsequently railroads, electricity, currency notes[17], money orders, photographs etc. and so forth were invented. If someone then asks us to prove the legality of these things from the sayings of the Companions, the Successors (*Tābi`īn*), or Imām Abū Hanīfa 鐵, or, prove their legality from *Hidāya*, *al-Dur al-Mukhtār*, or even '*Ālamgirī*, *Tahtāwi*, and *Rad al-Muhtār*, or let alone all these, show us the rulings from the books of Shah Abdul 'Azīz[18] 鐵, then the

---

[17] Currency notes were a contemporary issue in the lifetime of the author 鐵. Imām Ahmad Ridā Khān wrote a *Fatwā* on the status of paper money during his second pilgrimage in 1905 CE entitled *Kifl al-Faqih al-Fahim fi Ahkam Qirtas al-Darahim* [Guarantee of the Discerning Jurist on Duties relating to Paper Money]. The Muftī of the Hanafiyya in Makkah the Ennobled slapped his thigh while reading this book and exclaimed, "Where was Jamāl ibn Abdullāh 鐵 [i.e. the former Muftī of the Hanafiyya in Makkah] that he could not see this clear proof?" (*Malfuzat*, 2:184). This book along with *Al-Dawla al-Makkīyya bi al-madda al-ghaybiyya* [The Makkan Realm on the Matter of the Unseen] and *Husām al-Haramayn* [The Sword of the Sacred Sanctuaries] received immense praise and commendation.

[18] Shāh 'Abd al-'Azīz ad-Dehlawī 鐵 left this mundane world in 1823 before a single kilometre of railway line was laid in India. The author is fleshing out the sheer stupidity of the opponents argument, which hinges on wrongly accusing Muslims of unbelief (*Kufr*), innovation (*Bid'ah*), and idolatry (*Shirk*) simply because *Qiyām* and *Mawlid* occurred after the time of the Companions and the Successors (*Tābi`īn*). If we rely on their criteria, then every new invention after the time of the *Salaf* should be classified as *Bid'ah* and *Shirk*. Ironically, the detractors do not mind standing in a crowded railway-car or subway train, yet they detest the idea of standing up (*Qiyām*) out of respect for the Messenger of Allāh 鐵 during the celebration of his blessed birth (*Mawlid*).

only word to describe such a person is "stupid," because all of these developments in human history obviously occurred **after** the blessed lifetimes of the illustrious authors of the above works. On the one hand, the opponents think *Arba'īn*, a book written in the thirteenth century, is absolutely reliable. Even though many of the specific legal rulings and injunctions (*Juz'iyyāt*) found within the pages of this book did not exist in the first three centuries of Islām! On the other hand, they demand evidence from the time of the Companions and the Successors (*Tābi'īn*) for standing (*Qiyām*) and *Mawlid*. This is totally incomprehensible.

Similarly, mentioning the Prophet's ﷺ two beloved uncles (Sayyidunā Hamzā ؓ and Sayyidunā Abbās ؓ) in the Friday sermon (*Khutba*) was something new. However, the scholars have praised it as a recommended (*Mandūb*) or desirable action.

It is in *al-Dur al-Mukhtār*, "It is desirable (*Mustahab*) to mention the names of the four caliphs and the two beloved uncles in the sermon."[19]

Shaykh Mujaddid Alf Thāni ؓ actually wrote a letter to a Muslim who delivers the Friday sermon (*Khatīb*) condemning him for not mentioning the four caliphs in his sermon and went on calling him spiteful (*Khabīth*). The same can be said about the custom of sending blessings and salutations (*Salawāt*) on the Beloved Prophet ﷺ after the ritual prayer, which was widespread in the two Holy Sanctuaries. It is in *al-Dur al-Mukhtār*, "The sending of salutations was introduced in Rabi' al-Awwal 781 AH on Monday after the 'Ishā prayer. Thereafter, it was introduced after the Friday call to prayer (*Adhān*). Ten years on it was introduced after all the daily prayers and it was made twice after Maghrib. All of

---

[19] *Al-Dur al-Mukhtār*, the book of Salāh, the chapter of *al-Jumu'ah*, Mujtaba'i press, Delhi, vol.1, p. 111.

these cases are new forms of desirable innovation (*Bid`ah Hasanah*)."[20]

We can find many such examples and also the *Juziyyāt* of the scholars at that time. The gatherings of *Mawlid* and standing up (*Qiyām*) during the remembrance of the Prophet ﷺ has been going on for centuries. To ask the permissibility of such gatherings through the Companions, the Successors (*Tabi`īn*) or the great scholars is ludicrous. We should seek evidence from the scholars in whose time these blessed gathering were introduced. For example, we should read books by the renowned Hāfidh ﷺ, Imām Ibn Hajar ﷺ, Imām Jalāluddīn Suyūtī ﷺ, Imām Qastalāni ﷺ regarding the gathering of *Mawlid*. Proofs for *Qiyām* should also be obtained from their irrefutable treatises.

THOSE WHO REJECT ONE OF THE FOUR SCHOOLS OF ISLĀMIC LAW [*GHAYR MUQALLIDĪN*] ARE THE FOLLOWERS OF THEIR EGO

All praise be to Allāh! This should be enough to convince the detractors and the enemies of the truthful. It should not concern us at all if they do not accept it. And how are they going to listen when they do not listen to their own scholars! Those who do not follow any of the four Imāms (*Ghayr Muqallidīn*) openly reject the great scholarly verdicts and *Ijtihād*, or personal effort of qualified legal reasoning, by the great Imāms such as Imām al-A'żam Abū Hanīfa ﷺ. Moreover, they deem the followers of such great Imāms misguided polytheists (*Mushrik*).

What value do the sayings of our Imāms have in the eyes of those who are followers (*Muqallidīn*) by name, yet through their

---

[20] *Al-Dur al-Mukhtār*, the book of Salāh, the chapter of al-Adhān, Mujtaba'i press, Delhi, vol.1, p. 64.

ignorance and arrogance do not even accept a single verse from the Holy Qur'ān or the Hadīth much like their counterparts, the *Ghayr Muqallidīn*? These crypto-Wahhābis profess to follow qualified scholarship (*Taqlīd*); they use the Qur'ān and the Ahādīth in order to appease the common folk so that they are unable to completely reject them. However, their official creedal statement (*Aqida*) is *Taqwiyat al-Imān* [Strengthening the Faith] by Molvi Ismāil ad-Dehlawī. He alleged that, "Whoever says, 'Allāh and His Prophet have enriched them' is a polytheist (*Muskrik*)." Yet the Holy Qur'ān says,

$$
\text{تَحْلِفُونَ بِٱللَّهِ مَا قَالُواْ وَلَقَدْ قَالُواْ كَلِمَةَ ٱلْكُفْرِ وَكَفَرُواْ بَعْدَ إِسْلَـٰمِهِمْ وَهَمُّواْ بِمَا لَمْ يَنَالُواْ وَمَا نَقَمُوٓاْ إِلَّآ أَنْ}
$$

$$
\text{أَغْنَـٰهُمُ ٱللَّهُ وَرَسُولُهُ مِن فَضْلِهِ فَإِن يَتُوبُواْ يَكُ خَيْرًا لَّهُمْ وَإِن يَتَوَلَّوْاْ يُعَذِّبْهُمُ ٱللَّهُ عَذَابًا أَلِيمًا فِى ٱلدُّنْيَا وَٱلْآخِرَةِ}
$$

$$
\text{وَمَا لَهُمْ فِى ٱلْأَرْضِ مِن وَلِىٍّ وَلَا نَصِيرٍ ۝}
$$

"And they meditated a plot which they were unable to carry out: this revenge of theirs was (their) only return for the bounty with which Allāh and His Messenger had enriched them out of His grace" (9:74).

THE DOCTRINE OF THE WAHHĀBIS STIPULATES THAT NO ONE IS SAFEGUARDED FROM *SHIRK*, NOT EVEN ALLĀH ALMIGHTY

The author of *Taqwiyat al-Imān* also said that Muslims were, "attributing their sons to false deities by giving them names such as: 'Abdun Nabī, 'Alī Bakhsh, Husayn Bakhsh, Pīr Bakhsh, Madār Bakhsh, Salār Bakhsh, Ghulām Muhyuddīn and Ghulām Muinuddīn etc., because this is a form of idolatry (*Shirk*)."[21]

Just keeping the name 'Muhammad Bakhsh' is polytheism (*Shirk*) even though the meaning of this name is not specified or fixed. This is because *Bakhsh* may mean "partner," [but no Muslim

---

[21] *Taqwiyat al-Imān*, chapter one, (Matba' 'alimi, Andrun Lohari Darwaza, Lahore), p. 19.

would give this name to his child with the intention of setting up a "Partner" with Allāh Most Pure. *Bakhsh* is an Urdu word that also means: "giving, imparting, bestowing; yielding; forgiving;—giver, bestower; and forgiver"]. And the Book of Allāh does not object to this meaning,

قَالَ إِنَّمَآ أَنَا۠ رَسُولُ رَبِّكِ لِأَهَبَ لَكِ غُلَـٰمًا زَكِيًّا ۝

"He [the Archangel Jibra'īl ﷺ] said [to Maryam ﷺ], 'I am only a messenger of your Lord. That I may give you a pure son'" (19:19).

In this verse, the Archangel Jibra'īl ﷺ is openly announcing to the blessed virgin Maryam ﷺ that *he* will **give** her a pure son. Must we now declare him a polytheist too as per the religion of Ismāil ad-Dehlawī (the author of *Taqwiyat al-Imān*)? The Holy Qur'ān mentioned this, thus it has approved this "Wahhābi-Shirk." Why then don't they classify the Holy Qur'ān as the book of *Shirk*? There are many other examples, by which the great Companions ﷺ, Scholars ﷺ, Prophets ﷺ, Angels ﷺ and Allāh Himself will not be safe from the Wahhābis' libellous verdict of *Shirk*! This issue has been dealt with very clearly in my other books.[22]

It is enough for us to ask the reader: Why do we need to fret ourselves, when the detractors won't listen? How can they listen to and accept the words of the scholars when they do not listen to anyone? May the discussion of this first issue turn the detractors towards the people of the Truth. (Allāh is the provider of ability and grace and onto Him do we depend and seek His help. And salutations and blessings upon His Beloved Prophet Muhammad and upon his Family and Companions.)

---

[22] Such as *Ikmāl al-Tāma 'Alā Shirk Siwā Bil Umūr al-'Āmma* or *Al-Amnu Wa al-'Ulā Li Na'itī al-Mustafā* ﷺ *Bi Dāfi'ī al-Balā* etc.

If Allāh Almighty gives us the ability then it is enough for the just, fair and impartial to understand that *Qiyām* (standing for the Prophet at the time of *Mawlid*) has been a Tradition throughout the Islāmic world and has been widely accepted by the great Gnostics and Scholars of Religion. There is no denial of this in the *Shari'ah* and denying without the denial of the *Shari'ah* is unacceptable!

$$\text{مَا تَعْبُدُونَ مِن دُونِهِ إِلَّا أَسْمَاءً سَمَّيْتُمُوهَا أَنتُمْ وَءَابَاؤُكُم مَّا أَنزَلَ اللَّهُ بِهَا مِن سُلْطَنٍ ۚ إِنِ الْحُكْمُ إِلَّا لِلَّهِ ۚ أَمَرَ أَلَّا تَعْبُدُوٓا۟ إِلَّا إِيَّاهُ ۚ ذَلِكَ الدِّينُ الْقَيِّمُ وَلَكِنَّ أَكْثَرَ النَّاسِ لَا يَعْلَمُونَ ۝}$$

"There is no judgement but of Allāh" (12:40).

And unlawful (*Harām*) is that which is made unlawful (*Harām*) by Allāh. And those things, which He has not condemned, are permitted for you.[23]

The great scholars and jurists of the two Holy Sanctuaries, Makkah the Ennobled [*Mukarrama*] and Madinah the Illumined [*Munawwarah*] have practiced, acknowledged and approved this act. They did not call it forbidden (*Harām*), but described it as a desirable act (*Mustahab*), may Allāh send His salutations on the illuminator of the two Holy Cities and upon his Children and Family.

---

[23] *Jāmi' al-Tirmidhī*, the chapter on clothing, Ma Jā'a Fi Lubs al-Farra, (Āmīn company, Delhi) vol. 1, p.206.
Sunan Ibn Mājah, the chapter on food, Akl al-Jibn wa al-Saman, (H.M Saeed Company, Karachi), p. 249.
Al-Mustadrak Li al-Hākim, the chapter on food, Dar al-Fikr, Beirut, vol.4, p. 115.
It is also in *al-Bukhārī*, "O you who believe! Do not make unlawful the good things which Allāh has made lawful for you"(60:139).

Chapter Two: What the Muslims Deem Good

The distinguished scholar Imām 'Alī ibn Burhān al-Dīn al-Halabī ﷺ has said that standing (Qiyām) is a good innovation (Bid`ah Hasanah) in his renowned book Insān al-`Uyūn. He further states:

"Indeed the validity of standing up out of respect when the blessed remembrance takes place is taken from the practice of the great Jurist of Islām, Imām Taqi al-Millati wad-Dīn as-Subkī ﷺ, who is 'the Leader of the Leaders' (Imām of the Imāms) of Religion and Piety. The scholars of the time followed him in this practice. Imām as-Subkī ﷺ (d 756 AH/1355 CE) has written in at-Tabaqāt al-Kubrā that a large group of scholars gathered around him when Imām as-Sarsarī's (d. 656 AH/1258 CE) ode in praise of the Prophet ﷺ was being recited. The ode contained verses such as:

If the praise of the Chosen One was to be written in gold,
On a silver page with the finest script,
it would still be insufficient,
and all those who have reverence for this great Prophet,
at the time of his remembrance,
will stand up out of his respect
or will sit up on their knees

19

Upon hearing the verse in which the poet fervently urged the audience to stand at the time of the Prophet's auspicious remembrance ﷺ all of the scholars stood in reverence and found an immense tranquillity in that gathering. Imām al-Halabī ؊ states that "examples such as these are enough to be acted upon."[24]

I say: This venerable poet, Imām as-Sarsarī ؊, who wrote these choice lines, has been called "the *Hassān*[25] of his time and a true devotee of the Prophet ﷺ" by none other than 'Allāma Muhammad ibn 'Alī al-Shāmī ؊, whom the detractors use as a point of reference. This is written in *Subul al-Hudā wa al-Rashād*[26]. Moreover, Imām as-Subkī ؊ is such a personality whose greatness is obvious, up to the extent, that the leader of the detractors, Nazir Husain ad-Dehlawī, in one of his stamped scholarly verdicts (*Fatāwā*), acknowledged him as "the great Imām and the eminent Mujtahid by consensus." What's more, the scholars at the time of this great Imām followed him in this practice which is more than enough for the followers of the Pious Predecessors (*Salaf*). All praise be to Allāh! Did you not read at the end of the passage quoted from *Insān al-'Uyūn* what Imām al-Halabī ؊ wrote? He said: "Examples such as these are enough to be acted upon."

---

[24] *Insan al-'Uyūn Fi Sirat al-Āmīn al-Ma'mūn*, [*Tasmiyyatihi Muhammadan wa Ahmada*], Dar Ihya al-Turath al-'Arabi, Beirut, vol.1, p. 84.

[25] Hassān ibn Thābit ؊ was an Arabian poet and one of the companions of Prophet ﷺ. He was born in Madinah the Illumined (*Munawwarah*) and was a member of the Banū Khazraj tribe. In his youth, he travelled to al-Hirah and Damascus, then settled in Madinah, where, after the advent of Muhammad ﷺ, he accepted Islām and wrote poems in defence of him. He was one of the best poets of the time, who would often win poetry competitions and the like. He was a prime example of how the early Muslims were able to use their pre-Islāmic talents for the cause of Islām.

[26] *Subul al-Hudā wa al-Rashād Fī Sīrat Khair al-'Ibād*, the chapter *Fi Wad'ihi wa al-Nūr al-Ladhī Kharaja Minhu*, vol. 1, p. 344.

The book of the renowned Gnostic, Imām as-Sayyid Ja'far ibn Hasan ibn 'Abd al-Karīm al-Barzanjī ﷺ, entitled `Aqd al-Jawhar Fi Mawlid al-Nabī al-Azhar ﷺ, is a well-known book in two Holy Sanctuaries, and in other Islāmic states. The detractors like to cite Mawlānā Rafi'uddeen ﷺ, but he has praised this book and its author in *Tarīkh al-Haramayn*. It is in this book:

"Indeed to stand up during the remembrance of the Beloved Prophet ﷺ has been classified as a 'desirable act' (*Mustahsan*) by the scholars of *Riwāyah* and *Dirāyah*[27] so glad-tidings (*Tūba*) to those whose aim is honouring the Prophet ﷺ."[28]

Sayyidī Ja'far ibn Ismāil ibn Zain al-'Ābidīn `Alawī Madanī ﷺ wrote a very detailed commentary on the aforementioned book in *Al-Kawkab al-Azhar 'Alā 'Aqd al-Jawhar*.

The great Traditionalist (*Muhaddith*) and Jurist, Mawlānā Uthman ibn al-Hasan ad-Dimyātī ﷺ, writes in his treatise *Ithbāt al-Qiyām*, "To stand up at the time of mentioning the blessed birth of the beloved Prophet ﷺ out of respect is indeed a desirable (*Mustahab*) and good (*Mustahsan*) act. Whoever practises this will attain great blessings and merits. This is because this is a sign of respect and for whom? For the generous Prophet ﷺ through whom Allāh Almighty gave us refuge from the darkness of evil and placed us

---

[27] There are two disciplines that scholars employ before determining the proper use of a Hadīth. One is called *Riwāyah* and the other is called *Dirāyah*. The scholars of Hadīth focus essentially on *Riwāyah*, which helps determine the authenticity of the chain of narrators of a Hadīth. The scholars of Islāmic jurisprudence (*Fiqh*) use the tools of *Dirāyah* to determine how a Hadīth will be used in reaching a conclusion, taking into account the whole spectrum of Islāmic knowledge.

[28] `Aqd al-Jawahir Fi Mawlid al-Nabi al-Azhar (Urdu version), Jami'at Islāmiyyah, Lahore pp.25-26.

into the light of guidance and through whom He saved us from the fires of ignorance and moved us into the gardens of knowledge and understanding. Thus to respect him is to run towards the felicity of Allāh Almighty and to manifest the greatest Sign of Allāh, the Glorified (*Sha`āir Allāh*). *"That (is the command). And whoso respects the signs of Allāh, then it is from the piety of hearts"* (22:32). *"And whoso respects the sacred things of Allāh, then it is good for him with his Lord"* (22:30).[29]

Then after providing proofs he states, "...in other words, from all this evidence we understand that to stand up at the time of mentioning the miraculous birth of the Prophet 🕌 is *Mustahab*. This is a symbolic act that signifies respect for the Prophet 🕌. No one should argue that standing (*Qiyām*) is an innovation (*Bid`ah*) as not all innovations are rejected. This is also the answer given by Imām al-Muhaqqiq al-Walī Abū Dhar`ah al-`Irāqi 🕌. When he was asked whether celebrating *Mawlid* is *Mustahab* or disliked (*Makrūh*) and whether it has any proofs or was it invented by the scholars, he replied by saying that the banquet (*Walīma*) and feeding people is always *Mustahab*, then what can be said if these acts are merged with the happiness of the arrival of the Prophet in this glorious month. Even though we have not found any concrete evidence from our predecessors, but it does not make it a bad innovation, as many innovations are *Mustahab*, actually some of them are necessary (*Wājib*) if there is no deficiency attached to it. May Allāh give us the ability."

THERE IS CONSENSUS AND AGREEMENT AMONGST THE AHL AL-SUNNAH WA AL-JAMĀ'AH THAT *QIYĀM* IS A GOOD ACT

Then he states, "Indeed there is consensus and agreement amongst the Ahl al-Sunnah Wa al-Jamā'ah from the Community

---

[29] *Ithbāt al-Qiyām*, Imām ad-Dimyātī

(*Ummah*) of Prophet Muhammad 🌸 that standing (*Qiyām*) is a good act. And indeed our Beloved Prophet 🌸 has said, 'Truly Allāh does not gather my followers on misguidance'" (*Ibn Mājah*).

Imām 'Allama Madalqi 🌸 states, "It has become the norm among the people that when the religious singer (*Maddāh*) arrives at the birth of the Beloved Prophet 🌸, they all stand which is a good innovation as it signifies happiness and respect. (This has been transmitted by Imām ad-Dimyātī 🌸)."[30]

'Allāma Abū Zayd 🌸 writes in *Risālat al-Mawlid*, "It is righteousness to stand up during the observance of the birth of the Prophet 🌸."[31]

TO EXPRESS JOY, READ THE *MAWLID* AND TO FEED THOSE IN ATTENDANCE IS *MUSTAHAB*

Khātam al-Muhaddithīn Zayn al-Haram 'Ayn al-Karam Sayyid Ahmad Zayn Dahlān al-Makkī 🌸 writes in his book *Al-Durar al-Saniyyah Fī al-Radd 'ala al-Wahābiyyah*:

"What signifies respect for the Prophet 🌸 is to show delight on the day of his birth, narrating the story of his *Mawlid* on that night, standing up during narration of his blessed birth, offering food, and other good things that Muslims usually do. All these actions are related to displaying honour and respect for the Prophet 🌸. Many books have been written upon this subject and the issues which relate to this subject. Many scholars made special

---

[30] Ibid.
[31] *Risālat al-Mawlid*

preparations for it and wrote books filled with clear evidence and proofs, thus there is no need to prolong this subject."[32]

Shaykh al-Mashā'ikh Khātam al-Muhaqqiqin Imām al-'Ulamā Sayyid al-Mudarrisīn Muftī al-Hanafiyya bi Makkah al-Mahmiyya, our Master, Shaykh Jamāl ibn Abdullāh 'Umar al-Makkī ﷾, writes in his *Fatāwā*, "A group of scholars has classified standing up at the time of remembering the blessed birth of the Prophet ﷺ as a good act (*Mustahsan*). Therefore it is a good innovation."[33]

Then transmitting from 'Allāma Anbari's ﷾ *Mourid al-Dham'ān* he further writes, "Imām as-Subkī and the rest of the gathering stood up. This is enough for us to act upon."[34]

Scholars such as Mawlānā Siddiq Ibn 'Abd al-Rahmān Kamāl ﷾ (the teacher of Haram), 'Allāma Sayyid Ahmad Zayn Dahlān al-Shāfi'ī ﷾, Mawlānā Muhammad ibn Muhammad Katabu al-Makkī ﷾ and Mawlānā Husain ibn Ibrāhīm al-Mālikī al-Makkī ﷾, etc. have all agreed upon the above-mentioned verdict written by 'Allāma Jamāl ibn Abdullāh 'Umar ﷾ may Allāh benefit us from their knowledge.

Mawlānā Husain ibn Ibrāhīm ﷾, whom we mentioned above, writes in another place, "Many scholars have classified it as a good act as it is incumbent upon us to honour the Prophet ﷺ."

---

[32] *Al-Durar al-Saniyyah fi al-Radd 'ala al-Wahhābiyyah*, the chapter in the necessity of respecting the Prophet ﷺ, Dar al-Shafaqa, Istanbul Turkey, p.18.
[33] *Fatāwā* of Jamal ibn 'Umar al-Makkī
[34] Ibid.

THE SOUL OF THE PROPHET ﷺ IS PRESENT

The Muftī of the Hanbalī school, Mawlānā Muhammad ibn Yahyā al-Hanbalī ﷺ, writes, "Indeed to stand up at his (the Prophet's ﷺ) remembrance is necessary as the soul of the Prophet is present, thus we need to honour and respect him at that time."

I say: The word "necessary" is referring to the emphasis given by the scholar like a person says to his friend, "Your right is 'necessary' upon me." This type of saying is common among the Arabs as it is evident to those who are well-versed with their language. And about the soul of the Prophet ﷺ being present, then one should read the analytical view written by my blessed father ﷺ in his book *Idhāqat al-Āthām*. Mawlānā 'Abdullāh ibn Muhammad ﷺ, the Muftī of the Hanafī school, states, "Many scholars have deemed it as a good act."[35]

THE PERMISSIBILITY OF *QIYĀM* HAS COME DOWN THROUGH A CONTINUOUS CHAIN OF SCHOLARS

The Master of our Masters, the great Traditionalist (*Muhaddith*) and Jurist, Shaykh 'Abdullāh Sirāj al-Makkī ﷺ, the Hanafī Muftī, writes, "Standing (*Qiyām*) has come down to us through a continuous chain. No scholar has ever denied its legitimacy and thus it becomes *Mustahab*. And who else is worthier of respect than our beloved Prophet ﷺ? It is enough for us that the Hadīth of Abdullāh ibn Mas'ūd ﷺ states, 'Whatever the Muslims consider right is right in the judgement of Allāh.'"[36]

Similarly, Muftī Umar ibn Abū Bakr al-Shāfi'ī ﷺ also expressed its legitimacy and regarded it as *Mustahab*.

---

[35] *Fatāwā 'Ulamā al-Haramayn.*
[36] Ibid.

Fatāwā 'Ulamā al-Haramayn has been endorsed by grand Ulāma such as:

- the Muftī of Makkah, Mawlānā Muhammad ibn Husayn al-Kutbī al-Hanafī 🌸,
- Ra'īs al-'Ulamā Shaykh Mawlānā Jamāl al-Hanafī 🌸,
- Muftī Mawlānā Husain ibn Ibrahīm al-Makkī al-Mālikī 🌸,
- Sayyid al-Muhaqqiqīn Shaykh Mawlānā Ahmad ibn Zayn al-Shāfi'ī 🌸,
- the lecturer in the Prophet's 🌸 Mosque, Mawlānā Muhammad ibn Muhammad Gharb al-Shāfi'ī 🌸,
- Mawlānā 'Abd al-Karīm ibn 'Abd al-Hakīm al-Hanafī 🌸,
- the great jurist Mawlānā 'Abd al-Jabbār Hanbalā Basarā 🌸, who migrated to Madinah the Illumined (*Munawwarah*) from Basra, and
- Mawlānā Ibrāhīm ibn Khiyār al-Husayni al-Shāfi'ī al-Madanī 🌸.

I have seen this *Fatāwā* and seen their stamps with my own eyes. I had this *Fatāwā* for a very long time in which there are in-depth discussions around controversial subjects; it proves that the reasoning of the Wahhābi sect is erroneous and flawed through solid evidence.

It is in the same *Fatāwā*: "It is a virtuous action (*Mustahsan*) to stand up at the time of the remembrance of the birth of the Beloved Prophet 🌸 as mentioned in *Insān al-'Uyūn* (better known as *Sīrah Halabiyya*). 'Allāma Barzanjī 🌸 writes in *Risālat al-Mawlid*, 'According to the scholars of jurisprudence (*Fiqh*) and Hadīth it is *Mustahab* to stand up during the remembrance of the blessed birth as it is an expression of happiness for the one, whom respect and reverence is incumbent upon us'.[37] In addition, to label it as forbidden (*Harām*) due to a lack of evidence from the Ahādīth is false. It is in *'Ain an-'Ilm*, 'Anything for which there is no prohibition in the *Shari'ah* and that action has become a common practice in the time of the Pious Predecessors (*Salaf*) then it should be regarded as good (*Hasan*), even if it is *Bid'ah*.[38] I say, there is evidence to support this point in the Hadīth of Abdullāh ibn Mas'ūd ؆ in which he states, 'Whatever the Muslims consider right is right in the sight of Allāh'[39] and in the Hadīth, 'Deal with the Muslims in accordance to their customs and habits' (Narrated by Imām Hākim ؆, who said this Hadīth meets the conditions of Imām al-Bukhārī ؆ and Imām Muslim ؆)."[40]

THE PROOF OF *QIYĀM* FROM *IHYĀ*

Imām al-Ghazzālī ؆ states in *Ihyā*, "The fifth manner is to be consistent with the customs and traditions of the people. When a person stands up in spiritual ecstasy (*Wajd*) without boasting or he stood up without spiritual ecstasy out of his own choice, then all the people should join him and stand up; this is the manner of companionship (*Suhba*). In addition, every nation has its own tradition, and to deal with it accordingly is necessary like mentioned in (the aforementioned) Hadīth, especially when the traditions (or customs) are good practices and they delight the heart. To say it is an innovation (*Bid'ah*) and not proven from the Companions [is incorrect]. I challenge the one who said that the ruling of permissibility is only proven by the Companions? A 'bad

---

[37] *'Aqd al-Jawhar Fī Mawlid al-Nabī al-Azhar Li al-Barzanjī* (Urdu version), Jāmiah Islāmiyya Lahore, pp.25-26.

[38] *'Ayn al-'Ilm*, the chapter in *al-Samt wa Āfāt al-Lisān*, Amrat press Lahore, p.412.

[39] *Al-Mustadrak Li al-Hākim*, the chapter on *Ma'rifat al-Sahāba*, Dar al-Fikr, Beirut, vol.3, p. 78.

[40] *Itihāf al-Sādat al-Muttaqīn*, with reference to al-Hākim, the book on *al-Simā' wa al-Wajd*, chapter two stance three, Dār al-Fikr, Beirut, v.6, p. 572.

innovation' is that which contradicts the Sunnah, and there have been no prohibitions as regards to these actions. The same is true for all those customs which aim to delight people. And when one group of scholars have agreed upon it, then the best option is to join them (in agreement) except in those customs about which an explicit prohibition is stated and there is no room of opinion."[41]

TYPES OF INNOVATION (BID'AH)

Lastly, scholarly verdicts have been compiled in *Rawdat al-Na'īm* that describe the merits of *Mawlid* mentioned by the scholars of Madinah the Illumined (*Munawwarah*), it states:

"In conclusion, to feed the people, to narrate the incidents of the blessed birth, to give charity and distribute wealth, to stand up during the remembrance of the blessed birth of the blessed Prophet 鬈, and to shower rose petals, burn incense, to recite the Holy Qur'ān, to decorate one's house, to send salutations (*Salawāt*) upon the Holy Prophet 鬈, to express joy and happiness are all indeed *Mustahab* and good innovations. This is because not all innovations are forbidden; in fact, some are actually necessary like establishing proofs against the deviants or learning Arabic Grammar to aid in understanding the Qur'ān and the Ahādīth. Sometimes the innovations are *Mustahab* like establishing Islāmic Schools (*Madrasah*) and sometimes they are permissible like eating a variety of delicious foods and wearing different types of clothing. This has been mentioned by Imām al-Munāwi 鬈 in *Sharh Jāmi' Sagīr*, quoting from Imām an-Nawawi 鬈. Thus the only person who will argue with the above is going to be an innovator himself. We should not pay any attention to him as he should be punished by the Islāmic ruler."

---

[41] *Ihyā al-'Ulūm*, the book on *al-Sama' wa al-Wajd*, chapter two stance three, Matba' al-Mashhad al-Husaynī, Cairo, v.2, p.305.

This *Fatāwā* has been endorsed by more than thirty Scholars including Mawlānā 'Abd al-Jabbār ﷺ and Ibrāhīm ibn Khiyār ﷺ.

WHAT THE MUSLIMS DEEM GOOD IS ALSO GOOD IN THE JUDGMENT OF ALLĀH

Concerning the desirability of *Mawlid* and *Qiyām*, the *Fatāwā* of the scholars of Makkah the Ennobled (*Mukarrama*) states: "Thus the denier of the blessed gathering and *Qiyām* is an innovator of an evil innovation. This is because he has denied that which is virtuous in the sight of Allāh and the Muslims as mentioned in the Hadīth narrated by Abdullāh ibn Mas'ūd ﷺ, 'Whatever the Muslims consider right is right in the judgement of Allāh.'"

In this Hadīth, the word "Muslims" refers to the pious Muslims, that is the pious scholars. These actions have been classified as desirable by the scholars of Arabia, Egypt, Syria, Rome, and Andalusia etc. Therefore, there is a consensus, and any ruling that has been proven through consensus is righteousness and not falsehood. The Prophet of Allāh ﷺ has said, "Truly Allāh does not gather my followers over misguidance" (*Ibn Mājah*). Thus, the Islāmic ruler should punish the denier. And Allāh knows the best.

THE ENDORSEMENT OF THE *FATĀWĀ* BY MORE THAN 45 SCHOLARS

This *Fatāwā* has been endorsed by the likes of Sayyid al-'Ulamā Ahmad Dahlān ﷺ (the Shāfi'i Muftī), our Master Sirāj al-Fudalā Mawlānā 'Abd al-Rahmān Sirāj ﷺ (the Hanafi Muftī), Mawlānā Hasan ﷺ (the Hanbali Muftī), Mawlānā Muhammad Sharqi ﷺ (the Mālikī Muftī) and 45 other scholars.

Allāma Nāsir ibn 'Alī ibn Ahmad ﷺ in the *Fatāwā* of the scholars of Jeddah was the first Muftī to answer questions regarding the

Mawlid gatherings, *Qiyām*, fixing a specified day for it, decorating the place of gathering, to apply perfume, recitation of the Qur'ān and expressing happiness and joy. He writes, "A gathering in which all of the aforementioned things take place is good. No one shall deny its correctness except he who has one of the branches of hypocrisy in his heart. And how is it possible to deny it when Allāh Almighty says, '*And whoso respects the signs of Allāh, then it is from the pity of hearts'* (22:32)."

Mawlānā 'Abbas ibn Ja'far ibn as-Siddīq ﷺ writes, "The answer given by the grand Shaykh (Allāma Nāsir ibn 'Alī ibn Ahmad) is correct. None shall deny it except an open hypocrite. All acts mentioned in the question are good and why shouldn't they be, when all of these things express the honour of the Beloved Prophet ﷺ. May Allāh not deprive us from seeing him in this world and nor from his intercession in the Hereafter and whosoever denies it will be deprived from the two."

Mawlānā Ahmad Fattāh ﷺ writes, "It should be borne in mind that mentioning the blessed birth and miracles associated with the Prophet ﷺ and to gather to listen to them is indeed Sunnah. However, the present manner of commemorating as mentioned in the question and as observed in the two Sanctuaries is a good and desirable innovation (*Bidátun Hasanatun Mustahabbatun*). The commemorator shall be rewarded and the denier shall be punished."

Mawlānā Muhammad ibn Sulaymān ﷺ also writes, "Yes! The remembrance of the birth and to listen to the blessed birth is Sunnah. To commemorate as a congregation in which people stand up etc. is a good and desirable innovation, virtuous and beloved to Allāh Almighty. This is because of the Hadīth of Abdullāh ibn Mas'ūd ﷺ, 'Whatever the Muslims consider right is right in the judgement of Allāh.' The Muslims of the past until this day, the scholars and the Sufi saints (*Awliyā*) deemed it good without any defect. No one shall deny this virtuous act except he who wants to prohibit goodness and virtue, and this is the work of the Satan, the accursed."

Mawlānā Ahmad Jalīs ❀ writes, "Praise be to Allāh and salutations on the Chosen One (*Mustafā*) ❀. Yes! The mentioning of the miraculous birth and to describe the appearance (of the Beloved ❀) and to gather to listen to it, to decorate the house, to sprinkle rose water, to burn incense sticks, to fix the day, to stand up during the remembrance of the birth of the Prophet of Allāh ❀ and to feed the attendees, to distribute dates and to recite a few verses of the Holy Qur'ān are all acts of virtue. And Allāh Knows the Unseen."

Mawlānā Muhammad Sālih ❀ writes, "The Community (*Ummah*) of the Prophet of Allāh ❀ from the Arabs, Egypt, Syria, Rome, Andalusia and the entire Islāmic world are unanimous regarding its desirability and its goodness."

Similar verdicts have been written and endorsed by the likes of Ahmad ibn 'Uthmān ❀, Ahmad ibn 'Ajlān ❀, Muhammad Sadqa ❀ and 'Abd al-Rahīm ibn Muhammad az-Zabīdī ❀. Mawlānā Yahyā ibn Akram ❀ writes in *Fatāwā Jeddah*, "The scholars have written books on this subject and have recommended it and no one will dispute it except an innovator. The judge should punish him."

'Allāma 'Alī al-Shāmī ❀ writes, "No one will argue about this except one whose heart has been sealed by Allāh and indeed the scholars of Ahl al-Sunnah have mentioned that this act is a virtuous and a desirable deed."

Mawlānā 'Alī ibn Abdillāh ※ states, "The only one who will have any doubts about this is the one who is an innovator worthy of punishment."

Mawlānā 'Alī Tahān ※ writes, "It is desirable (*Mustahab*) to read the *Mawlid* and to stand during its recitation. Whoever denies it is stubborn and he has not understood the status of the Prophet ※."

Mawlānā Muhammad ibn Dāwud ibn 'Abd al-Rahmān ※ writes, "It is *Mustahab*. The one who practices it will be rewarded and only an innovator will deny its permissibility."

Mawlānā Muhammad ibn 'Abdillāh ※ writes, "To recite the *Mawlid*, and to stand up during the remembrance of the birth of the Prophet ※ and everything else that has been mentioned in the question are all ways of honouring the Prophet of Allāh ※, and who else is worthy of respect besides him ※?"

Mawlānā Ahmad ibn Khalīl ※ writes, "This is a true means of honouring the Prophet of Allāh ※. Therefore the Islāmic judge is ordered to rebuke and punish the one who rejects it."

Mawlānā 'Abdur Rahmān ibn 'Alī al-Hadramī ※ writes, "The scholars have deemed standing during the remembrance of the birth of the Prophet ※ as desirable and virtuous, as it is a mark of respect for him. And anything that is a means of expressing his love and exaltation should be made compulsory. No one shall deny this fact except the one who is an innovator and gone astray from the true path of Ahl al-Sunnah. No true Muslim will heed the detractor's deviant words and the judge should penalise him."

In short, the evidence from the books and statements of the scholars are present in which more than a hundred endorsements of the scholars are included. And the endorsements of the scholars of India are written in *Risalah Gāyat al-Marām*, which includes more than fifty stamped verdicts and certifications.

Now the just should ponder upon this fact: Is the agreement of the scholars of Makkah the Ennobled (*Mukarrama*), Madinah the Illumined (*Munawwarah*), Jeddah, Hadidah, Rome, Syria, Egypt, Dimyat, Yemen, Zabid, Basra, Hadramawt, Aleppo, Abyssinia, Barzanj, Bara', Kurd, Dagestan, Andalusia, and India not an explicit proof? Or, Allāh forbid, are personalities of such calibre from the time of Imām Taqi al-Millati wad-Dīn as-Subkī (d. 765 AH/1355 CE) ﷺ till today misguided innovators? And will they deem these luminaries as people who classify a bad innovation as good? O critic! Don't be too stubborn. We will show you the way! Empty your heart from all worldly-thoughts, close your eyes, put your head down and imagine that all these great scholars are present at one time and place in a very dignified setting. The question is then posed to them, and all these eminent scholars answer with one voice, "Indeed it is *Mustahab!* Who is there to deem it wrong? Let him come to us!" At that time, imagine the awe and magnitude of such scholars and see what courage some of those Indian-deniers have in front of these august personalities and let us see if they can even open their mouths in their presence!

When a lion leaves the jungle even a limping fox will then come out to hunt.

He who is audacious enough should ask, "Who are these scholars? We do not accept their statement. Is their statement even valid as evidence?"

33

Even so, let us assume that all these luminaries erred in mentioning the correct ruling. But were they mistaken, Allāh forbid, in the narrations? Now read again the aforementioned [imaginary] statement, then see how many scholars have mentioned that there is consensus (*Ijmā'*) upon the desirability of this deed [from their actual declarations quoted above]. Has the consensus of the scholars been rejected too and is it no longer regarded as evidence?

FOLLOWING THE VIEW OF THE MAJORITY

Okay, forget all this. Let us assume that consensus (*Ijmā'*) has been "broken" due to the criticism of a few Indian scholars, who wrote with unprecedented liberty and total impunity [since Islāmic criminal law was abolished by the British Raj in the 1860s]. But how can we deny the majority-view (*al-Sawād al-'Adham*)?[42] The Prophet of Allāh ﷺ has said, "Follow the view of the majority. Whosoever stays on his own, will be thrown into the Hellfire on his own."[43] And also, "The wolf will only attack the sheep which is separated from its flock."[44]

Do justice! The verdict of Imām as-Subkī ؓ and of the scholars of his time was enough for the Muslims to prove the permissibility of standing, after which there is no need of any further evidence, as mentioned by Jalīl 'Alī ibn Burhān Halabī ؓ and 'Allāma Ambārī ؓ. The common folk and the elite have practised *Qiyām* for hundreds of years. Thousands of scholars and Sufi saints (*Awliyā*) have agreed upon its consensus. Despite all this, the critic

---

[42] Imām al-Shāfi'ī ؓ said: "We know that the people at large cannot agree on an error and on what may contradict the Sunnah of the Prophet ﷺ" (*Risala*).

[43] *Al-Mustadrak Li al-Hākim*, the chapter of al-'Ilm, Dār al-Firk, Beirut, v.1, pp.115-116.

[44] *Al-Sunan al-Kubrā*, the book of al-Salāh, the chapter of Fard al-Jamā'ah Fī Ghayr al-Jumu'ah 'Alā al-Kifāyah, Dār Sādir, Beirut, v.3, p.54.

does not accept it. What a pity! According to the doctrine (*Aqida*) of our opponents, all the scholars of the *Ummah* of the Prophet ﷺ must be looked upon as innovators, and in their view, these dissenting Indians alone are Muslims; these crypto-Wahhābis, who have been audacious because there is no Islāmic government in the Subcontinent!

This was a concise analysis on the permissibility of standing (*Qiyām*) as regards to only one proof [i.e. the Hadīth of Abdullāh ibn Mas'ūd ﷺ]. There are hundreds of other proofs which are proven from the Holy Qur'ān and the Ahādīth. The description of these evidences are found in the book of my blessed father, the crown of the 'Ulamā, the head of the Gnostics, my Master, my Guide, Mawlānā Muhammad Naqī 'Alī Khān al-Qādirī al-Barakātī ﷺ, namely, *Idhāqat al-Āthām Li Man'ī 'Amal al-Mawlid wa al-Qiyām*. The proofs within this book are more than enough and require no further elaboration. Glad tidings to the one who wants to read a just study and a very detailed enquiry about this subject for he will gain immense blessings from this book.

STANDING TO COMMEMORATE THE PROPHET'S BIRTH ﷺ IS ACTUALLY A SIGN OF RESPECT FOR HIM

Now a question could arise here: Why is a time specified for standing (*Qiyām*) during the remembrance of the Prophet's blessed birth ﷺ? The answer should be apparent. First of all, it has been the practice of the scholars for centuries. Second, these same scholars have stated that showing reverence for the Prophet ﷺ by commemorating his blessed birth is actually a mark of respect for him. Moreover, standing (*Qiyām*) is one of the ways we honour the arrival of an elite dignitary. Since the commemoration of the Prophet's birth ﷺ is the remembrance of his arrival to this world, this form of respect is more appropriate at that time.

Our sect, the Ahl al-Sunnah wa al-Jamā'ah, has attained a great share of Allāh's Mercy.

NAZĪR AHMAD SHĀHJAHĀN ĀBĀDĪ HAS INDIRECTLY DEEMED *QIYĀM* AS *MUSTAHAB*

The leader (*Imām*) of the detractors, Mawlānā Nazīr Ahmad Shāhjahān Ābādī, classified *Qiyām* as a bad innovation (*Bid'ah*). He has been given the title *Shaykh al-Kul fī al-Kul*, and was praised by Miyān Bashīr al-Dīn Qanujī in his book *Gāyat al-Kalām* with the words, "...the best among the research scholars and the reliability of the Muhaddithīn[45], Mawlānā Nazīr Ahmad Shāhjahān Ābādī is one of the greatest Sufi saints (*Awliyā*) and scholars of this era." This book attempts to prove the prohibition of *Qiyām*.[46] Yet Mawlānā Nazīr has unconsciously acknowledged the permissibility of standing and its desirability (*Istihbāb*) himself!

In the previous discussion, we mentioned how Imām as-Subkī 🕮 and his contemporaries stood up out of respect for the Chosen One 🕮 at the time of his remembrance. Mawlānā Nazīr cannot disagree with us, because his reliable source ('Allāma 'Alī al-Shāmī 🕮) has also mentioned this incident in his book *Subul al-Hudā wa al-Rashād*. Moreover, this same man has openly stated in one of his stamped verdicts (the original copy of which is present with me) that, "There is a consensus among the scholars regarding the *Ijtihād*[47] of Imām as-Subkī 🕮."

---

[45] *Zubdat al-Muhaqqiqīn wa 'Umdat al-Muhaddithīn*
[46] *Ghāyat al-Kalām*, by Bashīr al-Dīn Qanujī.
[47] *Ijtihād*: personal effort of qualified legal reasoning.

Imām Ibn Hajar ☙, the Mujtahid of Makkah the Ennobled, writes, "He is such an Imām upon whose dignity and *Ijtihād* there is a consensus."[48]

Note well that this 13th century "Mujtahid" (Mawlānā Nazīr) has also agreed that Imām as-Subkī ☙ is a Mujtahid. He also asserted in the aforementioned *Fatāwā* that, "When an Imām, whose *Ijtihād* is correct, acts upon something then we have to believe that his *Ijtihād* is a proof for that action, and the *Ijtihād* of a Mujtahid is indeed a legislative evidence (*Hujjat*)."

How can there be room for dispute in this debate when the act of *Qiyām* is proven by incontrovertible legislative evidence (*Hujjat*)? He went on to say that, "The school of a Mujtahid cannot be categorized as an innovation (*Bid'ah*) just as the four schools of Islāmic jurisprudence cannot be classified as misguidance. Whosoever violates this rule is surely a wretched innovator and a worshipper of monks (*Ahbār wa Ruhbān*). This is because a Mujtahid whether of the past or the present manifests the Orders of Allāh and does not prove them."

Now it is incumbent upon us to believe that a person who regards *Qiyām* as *Bid'ah* is "a wretched innovator and a worshipper of monks."

He further states, "Allāh creates the Mujtahid so that he can explain the ruling of a new issue (which has not been solved in the past). Thus to taunt the Mujtahid is reproaching the Qur'ān and the Ahādīth. And to mention the Hadīth, "He who innovates something in this matter of ours that is not of it will have it

---

[48] *Fatāwa Hadīthiyyam Matlab Fīmā Jarā Min Ibn Taymiyyah*, Matba' Jamāliyya, Egypt, p.85.

rejected (by Allāh)[49]" (*al-Bukhārī* and *Muslim*[50]), is firstly being deceitful and secondly inappropriate..."

For a lengthier analysis, to answer the criticisms of the detractors and to prove them wrong, one should study my book *al-Sārim al'Ilāhī 'Alā 'Amā'id al-Mashrab al-Wāhī*. I intended to falsify the *Fatwā* of Mawlānā Nazīr by the support and Mercy of Allāh Almighty, Inshā'Allāh. This book contains the confessions and admissions of the deviants' leaders.

---

[49] *Man Ahdatha...*

[50] In one version related by Muslim it reads, "He who does an act which we have not commanded, will have it rejected [by Allāh]."

Chapter Three: Point Counter-Point

An entire library could be filled with books discussing the details of this second issue. Our scholars ('*Ulamā*) from the Arab world and those from non-Arab lands have not left any deficiency in proving the truth and eradicating falsehood, especially the defender of the Sunnah, the eradicator of falsehood, the Proof (*Hujjat*) of Allāh on this earth, the miracle of the Prophet ﷺ, my beloved father, Mawlānā Naqī 'Alī Khān ؓ. He made a very detailed inquiry outlining several important points in his book *Usūl al-Rashād Li Qam'i Mabāni al-Fasād* after which there is no need of further clarification. Therefore, I am only going to mention some concise points in this section. If the reader is not completely satisfied with these points, then I am prepared to furnish him with more information. There is no might and power except from Allāh, the Almighty and All-Powerful.

POINT 1

All things in their original state are permissible, except for those things that are proven to be forbidden by the *Shari'ah*. This is especially true if the permissibility of those things is mentioned in the Holy Qur'ān or the Ahādīth. Conversely, the same rule applies if there is no textual evidence prohibiting it. So if a person claims that something is forbidden (*Harām*) or disliked (*Makrūh*), then he must support his claim with concrete evidence as there is no need to prove the permissibility of things, because of our default assumption about its originality. If there is no legislative evidence

39

to prove its impermissibility, then this *is* the very proof of its permissibility.

It is in *Jām'i Tirmidhī, Sunan Ibn Mājah, Mustadrak li Hākim,* narrated by Salmān Fārsi ❀ that the Beloved of Allāh ❀ has said, "Lawful (*Halāl*) is that which is made *Halāl* in the Qur'ān. Unlawful (*Harām*) is that which is made *Harām* by the Qur'ān. And what it remains silent about is forgiven."[51] In other words, one will not be penalised for acting upon things about which the Qur'ān is silent.

It is in *Mirqāt*, "This Hadīth proves the permissibility of things in their original state"[52] (*Anna al-Asla Fī al-Ashyā'ī al-Ibāhatu*).

Shaykh 'Abd al-Haqq Muhaddith ad-Dehlawī ❀ writes, "This evidence is proof that the original state of things is permissibility."[53]

Nasr ❀ narrates from Amīr al-Mu'minīn 'Umar ❀ in his *Kitāb al-Hujjah*, "Indeed Allāh Almighty has created you all. He knows your weaknesses and thus He sent amongst you His Prophet ❀. He also sent down His Book and He made the boundaries clear (*Hudūd*) and commanded you not to transgress the boundaries laid down by Him. He made certain things obligatory upon you

---

[51] *Jāmi' al-Tirmidhī*, the chapter on al-Libās, the chapter on Mā Ja'a Fī Lubs al-Farā, Amīn Company, Delhi, v.1, p.206.
Sunan Ibn Mājah, the chapters on food, the chapter on Akl al-Jubn wa al-Saman, A.M.Saīd Compnay, Karachi, p.249.
[51] *Al-Mustadrak Li al-Hākim*, the chapter on al-At'imah, Dār al-Firk, Beirut, v.4, p.115.
[52] *Mirqāt al-Mafātīh*, the chapter on al-At'imah, under Hadīth# 4228, al-Maktabat al-Habībiyyah, Koita, v.8, p.57.
[53] *Ashi'at al-Lam'āt*, the chapter on al-At'imah, chapter two, Hadīth#4228, Nūriya Razawiyya, Sikhar, v.3, p.506.

(*Fard*) so obey those obligations and He made certain things unlawful (*Harām*) so that you may abstain from those forbidden things. He left other things so that you do not neglect them forgetfully and so that you do not fall into difficulties. He has indeed left them as a mercy for you all."

Imām 'Ārif Billāh Sayyidī 'Abd al-Ghanī an-Nāblūsī ⬥ states, "Cautiousness is not that you accuse Allāh by stating certain things as forbidden (*Harām*) or disliked (*Makrūh*) as such things demand clear proof, but cautiousness is to regard things as permissible as this is their originality (*Asl*)."[54]

Mawlānā Mullā 'Alī al-Qārī ⬥ writes in *al-Iqtidā Bī al-Makhālif*, "The originality of things is permissibility, and this is definitely known. As for statements of *Harām* and *Makrūh* then it demands evidence to prove them from the Book of Allāh, the Hadīth, or from the consensus (*Ijmā'*) of the *Ummah*."

There is a myriad of textual evidence from the Holy Qur'ān, the Ahādīth of the Beloved Prophet ⬥ and the statements of our great scholars ('*Ulamā*) to prove this point. Up to the extent that even Mawlānā Nazīr wrote the following in his own endorsed verdict, "O Fool! Only Allāh and His Prophet ⬥ have the right to declare a certain thing permissible, then how is it a different matter when they say such a thing is impermissible? Tell me, if what you say is impermissible, then has Allāh and His Beloved Prophet ⬥ deemed it such?"

Thus from the above quote, there is no need for us to prove the permissibility of *Qiyām* and other seemingly controversial issues. The evidence for Sunnis is that the *Shari'ah* has not forbidden us

---

[54] *Rad al-Muhtār* with reference to al-Sulh bayn al-Ikhwān, the chapter on al-Ashriba, Dār Ihyā al-Turāth al-'Arabī, Beirut, v.5, p296.

from these acts. Therefore, for the opponents to ask us to produce evidence is completely ludicrous and according to the ruling of their own Mujtahid, it is utterly foolish!

Yes! When the detractors say it is *Harām* and impermissible then they should prove their point from the words of the Holy Qur'ān and the Ahādīth. And when they cannot prove it to be so, and Insha'Allāh, they will never be able to do so, then why do they find fault with the *Shari'ah*?

وَلَمَّا دَخَلُواْ عَلَىٰ يُوسُفَ ءَاوَىٰٓ إِلَيْهِ أَخَاهُ قَالَ إِنِّىٓ أَنَا۠ أَخُوكَ فَلَا تَبْتَئِسْ بِمَا كَانُواْ يَعْمَلُونَ ۝

Say, "Indeed those who fabricate lies against Allāh will never succeed"
(12:69).

POINT 2

To prove the legality of something from the generality ('*Umūm*) has been the practice from the time of the Companions till this day and age. In other words, when an act has been proven permissible by the *Shari'ah*, then it will be regarded as such wherever and whenever the act is executed till there is evidence to prevent us. For example, the generality of the remembrance of Allāh (*Dhikr*) is proven from the Qur'ān and the Ahādīth. Therefore to do *Dhikr* in any place, at any time, and in any position is permissible as there is no need for further evidence to prove this. However, the *Shari'ah* has restricted us from making *Dhikr* whilst relieving ourselves, and so it will be prohibited at that particular time.

So when a certain action is proven generally to be virtuous, then there is no need to seek evidence to prove its permissibility at a specified place and time as these specific moments come under that general ruling. Yes, of course, to regard an act impermissible at a particular time or during a specific setting demands evidence.

It is in *Musallam al-Thubūt*, "The usage of the generality by the scholars of the past and the present is well known." [55] Also in the same book, "Acting upon the general ruling demands its generality."[56]

It is in *Tahrīr al-Usūl* by Imām 'Allāma Ibn al-Humām ﷺ and in its commentary, "When the generality of an action is established, then this is enough to act upon it."

It is also in the *Fatāwā* of Mawlānā Nazīr, "When a ruling has been established by its generality (*'Umūm*) then it will remain upon its generality. The *'Ulamā* have sought evidence from the generality of issues from the time of the Companions till this day."

Now, the virtue of the *Dhikr* of Allāh is proven in the Qur'ān, *"And Remember Allāh in abundance"* (33:41).

And the remembrance of our beloved Prophet ﷺ and other Prophets ﷺ is the remembrance of Allāh. We remember them only because they are beloved and Prophets of Allāh Almighty. Together with all this, the remembrance of the Prophet ﷺ during the *Mawlid* is only through the narration of his unique qualities and status that Allāh the Exalted has given him. Now we may consider this narration as narrating a bounty, since Prophet Muhammad ﷺ is a wondrous personage, who has been bestowed a very exalted rank. So this will be like mentioning the verse, *"There are some whose ranks have been raised"* (2:253).

On the other hand, these narrations will also be a form of praising Allāh, Who bestowed His beloved ﷺ with such a lofty,

---

[55] *Musallam al-Thubūt*, Chapter Five, [*masalat Li 'Umūm as-Siyag*], Matba' Ansārī, Delhi, p.73.
[56] Ibid, p.119.

unattainable status. Then this will be like mentioning the verse, *"Glory be to Him Who took His slave..."* (17:1) or the verse, *"He is the One Who sent His Prophet with Guidance"* (9:33). Allāh Almighty says to His Beloved, *"And We have raised for you your remembrance"* (94:4).

Imām al-Qādī 'Iyād ﷺ writes under the above verse in his *al-Shifā* quoting from the Tafsīr of Sayyidī Ibn 'Atā ﷺ, "in other words, Allāh is saying to His beloved, 'I have made your remembrance part of My Remembrance. Thus, whosoever remembers you has remembered Me.'"[57]

The Muslims believe that the remembrance of the Chosen One (*Mustafā*) ﷺ is, in fact, the Remembrance of Allāh Almighty. According to the ruling of the generality, in whatever form he ﷺ is remembered it should be allowed and regarded as a virtuous deed. Thus, there is no need to prove the permissibility of remembering him during the *Mawlid*, or during the *Salawāt* after the 'Adhān. Yes! Whoever declares this action to be forbidden must back up his claim with legislative evidence.

Similarly, Allāh has (generally) commanded us to remember His bounties, *"Remember the bounties of your Lord in abundance"* (93:11). The birth of the Messenger of Allāh ﷺ is the root of all the bounties, and the remembrance of His bounties in abundance is the command of the Qur'ān. The remembrance of something in abundance can be achieved in a gathering in front of many people. This is the gathering of the *Mawlid*.

Moreover, the believers faith (*Imān*) hinges on his love and respect for the Prophet ﷺ. The virtue of this is mentioned in the Holy

---

[57] *Al-Shifā Bi Ta'rīf Huqūq al-Mustafā* ﷺ, chapter one, al-Matba' al-Sharikat al-Sahhāfiyya, v.1, p.15.

Qur'ān, "O Prophet! We have sent you as a witness, provider of glad tidings, and a clear warner. So that you (O believers!) believe in Allāh and His Prophet and honour him and respect him" (48:9). Also, "Whoever respects the Signs of Allāh then it is from the piety of the hearts" (22:32). And, "Whosoever respects the sacred ordinances of Allāh then that will be better for him in the sight of his Lord" (22:30).

Thus due to the generality of the verse, any manner that signifies respect for the Prophet ﷺ is virtuous and there is no need to demand proof for specific mannerisms of respect like standing. However, if there is an explicit prohibition from the *Shari'ah* regarding a specific mannerism then it is undoubtedly forbidden. For instance, a Muslim **cannot** prostrate before the Beloved of Allāh ﷺ, or take the name of the Prophet ﷺ instead of reading the *Takbīr* ("Allāhu Akbar"), whilst sacrificing an animal.

It is for this reason that Imām Ibn Hajar ؓ states in *Johar Munazzam*, "All modes of respect for the Prophet of Allāh ﷺ that are free from associating partners with Allāh are recommended according to those whose insight has been illuminated by Allāh Almighty."[58]

The believers began the practice of standing (*Qiyām*) as a mark of respect for the Prophet ﷺ, which is a desirable action, unless, of course, there is some proof from the *Shari'ah*, the Qurān, and the Hadīth that forbids it. And how will the detractors ever be able to prove this, since point two teaches us that *Qiyām* is proven from the verses of the Holy Qurān itself, what to speak of the Successors (*Tābi'īn*) or the Successors of the Successors (*Taba' Tābi'īn*).

---

[58] *Al-Jawhar al-Munadhdham*, the introduction in the Ādāb al-Safar, chapter one, al-Maktabat al-Qādiriyyah, Lahore, p.12.

POINT 3

We would like to ask the critics a few questions: Is an act only permissible or prohibited if it is mentioned explicitly in the Holy Qurān or the confirmed Hadīth? Or would it be sufficient if it comes under the general permissibility or prohibition of things? According to the first criterion that necessitates an explicit scriptural text it becomes obligatory upon them to prove the prohibition of *Mawlid* and *Qiyām* by the very word of the Qurān itself or from the books of Hadīth. And if the second criterion is sufficient for them as evidence, then why do they demand proof from us when these virtuous actions come under the generality of remembrance, respect and reverence?

POINT 4

All of the detractors and their associates are afflicted with this illness that if such and such a new deed is not mentioned in the Qurān or the Ahādīth and if it is found in such and such a time then it is permissible and if found after that time then it is misguidance. However, the rulings of the *Shari'ah* and the goodness of a deed are not bound by any particular point in time. Virtuous deeds regardless of when they are performed will remain virtuous, and immoral acts will remain immoral regardless of when they are acted upon. In the end, incidents like the assassination of Amīr al-Mu'minīn 'Uthmān ibn 'Affān ﷺ, the tragedy of Karbalā and Harra, the innovations of the Khawārij (the enemies of Sayydunā 'Alī ﷺ), the slanderous remarks of the Rawāfid (who were enemies of the Companions), the evils of the Nawāsib (those who hate the household of the Prophet ﷺ) and the immergence of Mu'tazilites were all found at the time of the blessed Companions. Will all these incidents be classified as virtuous, simply because they belong to that period? Allāh Forbid!

And what about those things that emerged after the time of the blessed Companions such as the establishment of Islāmic schools, books, rejoinders to evil innovations, imparting knowledge of Arabic grammar, and the methodology for practicing *Dhikr* plus other spiritual exercises initiated by the great Sufi saints (*Awliyā*), will they be classified as immoral acts?

The only criterion to distinguish between a virtuous and an immoral act is by the very essence of that deed. Any action whose goodness has been mentioned in the Qurān or Hadīth, explicitly or implicitly, is going to remain good wherever it is found. And any action which is disliked by the *Shari'ah*, explicitly or implicitly, is going to remain detested wherever and whenever it is found. The majority of the scholars have explained this very important ruling in their respective books even though the detractors refuse to accept this crucial point. You have already read the statement of Imām al-Walī Abū Dhar`ah al-`Irāqi ☀ that every new thing is not disliked as there are numerous innovations which are *Mustahab*, and some are actually *Wājib* so long as they do not contain anything which is against the *Shar'iah*.

Similarly, Hujjat al-Islām Imām al-Ghazzālī ☀ states: "[If someone says that something is] 'Not to be proven from the time of the Companions' [that person's assertion] does not prove prohibition, rather prohibition is when an innovation goes against the commandments of the Sunnah."[59]

He also writes in *Kīmiyā'i Sa'ādat*, "Though all these deeds are new and not proven to be the practices of the Companions or of their Successors (*Tābi'īn*), nevertheless they are not prohibited either. This is because there are many new things that are good. The only

---

[59] *Ihyā al-'Ulūm*, the book on *al-Sama' wa al-Wajd*, chapter two stance three, Matba' al-Mashhad al-Husaynī, Cairo, v.2, p.305.

prohibited innovation is that which is contrary to the teachings of the Sunnah."[60]

Scholars like Imām al-Bayhaqī ﷺ narrate from Imām al-Shāfi'ī ﷺ, "*Bid'ah* is of two kinds: praiseworthy innovation and blameworthy innovation. The first kind is good and should be implemented as it does not go against the *Shari'ah*. This kind of *Bid'ah* is not overlooked [m: it should be practiced]. The second kind is contrary to the Qur'ān, Aḥādīth, *Āthār* or the consensus (*Ijmā'*), and this is prohibited."[61]

Imām Ibn Hajar ﷺ writes in *Fath al-Bārī Sharh Sahīh al-Bukhārī*, "If an innovation comes under such a category which is liked in the *Shari'ah* then it is liked too. If it comes under such a category which is disliked in the *Shar'ah*, then it is prohibited. And if an innovation comes under neither of these two categories then it is permissible (*Mubāh*)."[62]

Now the opponent's claim that *Qiyām* and *Mawlid* are prohibited just because it was not practiced at the time of the Companions or the Successors (*Tābi'īn*) is erroneous. Yes! They will only be regarded as prohibited innovations when the detractors prove that the practices themselves are immoral. Otherwise if they fall under the category of praiseworthy innovation then they are good, and if they do not fall under the category of blameworthy innovation then they will remain permissible (*Mubāh*). And any *Mubāh* act practiced with a good intention is liked in the *Shari'ah* as mentioned in *Bahr al-Rā'iq*. Point four proves irrefutably that to demand proofs for these practices from the time of the

---

60 *Kīmiyā'ay al-Sa'ādat*, chapter two, *Intishārāt Ghanjīna*, Iran, pp.388-389.
61 *Al-Qawl al-Mufīd Li al-Shawkānī*, the chapter in *Ibtāl al-Taqliyya*, v.1, p.78.
62 *Fath al-Bārī*, the book on al-Tarāwīh, Mustafā al-Bābī, Egpyt, v.5, pp.156-157.

Companions or the Successors (*Tabi'īn*) is foolhardy. All praises is for Allāh!

POINT 5

In this point we will respond to the detractors favourite Hadīth, "The best of people are my century" (*Khayr al-Qurūni Qarnī*).[63] All praise belongs to Allāh! Our opponents cannot offer a tiny shred of evidence to support their claim from this Hadīth. The words of the Hadīth are, "The best of people are my century, then those that follow them, then those that follow the latter. After that there will come lies, betrayal, selfishness and people who will be eager to commit perjury when bearing witness[64]." So how does this tradition prove the prohibition of everything introduced **after** the first three centuries of Islāmic history, even though they come under the category of 'the originality of things' [ref: point one] or belong to 'the generality ('*Umūm*)' [ref: point two]? Whosoever says this should prove it from the words of this Hadīth. My friend! To believe that there was no evil during those first four hundred years of Islāmic history and that there is nothing worthwhile after that blessed time period is completely erroneous. Yes! There is no doubt that in those days there were God-fearing people who were pious and sincerely devoted to the Religion (*Dīn*), and thereafter we see tribulations and wickedness spreading everywhere. Whom is this wickedness amongst? Is it amongst those who are acquainted with true knowledge and love for the elite? Allāh Forbid! The scholars in every era have remained the centre of goodness.

In the past Islāmic knowledge was widespread and very few people were ignorant. Nevertheless, the ignorant masses followed

---

[63] *Jāmi' al-Tirmidhī*, the chapter on al-Shahādāt, Amīn Company, Delhi, v.2, p.54.
[64] This Hadīth is in *al-Bukhārī* and *Muslim* narrated by 'Abdullāh ibn Mas'ūd ﷺ.

the teachings of their scholars, therefore we saw less evil. This is because the foundations of Religion (*Dīn*) are intrinsically linked to true Islāmic knowledge. Thereafter we saw a decrease in knowledge and widespread ignorance. The ignorant people took to their own ways and so the tribulations and mischief appeared and multiplied. Now we see that the scholars of the past deemed *Qiyām* as *Mustahab*, and the rejecters patently refuse to follow them. Thus the mischief nowadays relates back to these ignorant people, and who would seek evidence from one bereft of true guidance and real knowledge? Our belief is not such that we deem as good whatever the ignoramus introduces into our Religion. Rather, it is understood by the words of our scholars' par excellence that whatever the eminent personalities have deemed *Mustahab* will be accepted as such whenever it was made *Mustahab*. This is because the scholars of the Religion (*Dīn*) can never be the centre of evil wherever and whenever they exist. All praise is for Allāh, the Lord of the Worlds.

POINT 6

If the praise of an era and the disapproval for it thereafter, as specified in the Hadīth ("The best of people are my century..."), necessitates that the innovations of the former era are good and those of the subsequent centuries are increasingly evil, then the Companions and the majority of the Successors (*Tabi'īn*) have not been saved from this. [Take for example the following Ahādīth that testify to the misfortune that will occur after the demise of the first three rightly-guided Caliphs ﷺ:]

Hadrat Anas ﷺ narrates, "The people of Banū al-Mustaliq sent me to the Prophet of Allāh ﷺ in order to ask him a question: 'Who should we give our alms-tax (*Zakāt*) to after you?' He replied, 'Give it to Abū Bakr ﷺ.' I then asked, 'What if a calamity befalls him?' He replied, 'Give it to 'Umar ﷺ.' Again I asked, 'What if a calamity befalls him?' He then said, 'Give it to `Uthmān ﷺ.' And again I inquired, 'What if a calamity befalls him?' The Prophet of Allāh ﷺ then said, 'If a calamity befalls `Uthmān ﷺ then woe to you. There will be misfortune forever.'"[65]

Narrated by Abū Nu'aym ﷺ in *al-Hilyah* and *al-Tabrānī* narrating from Sahal ibn Abī Hathma ﷺ in a long Hadīth:

The Prophet of Allāh ﷺ said, "When Abū Bakr ﷺ, 'Umar ﷺ and `Uthmān ﷺ pass away then if you can, you should depart this life."

Abū Nu'aym ﷺ also narrated that the Messenger of Allāh ﷺ has said, "When I and Abū Bakr ﷺ, 'Umar ﷺ and `Uthmān ﷺ leave this world then if it is possible you should depart this life."[66]

Imām al-Tabrānī ﷺ narrates in *al-Kabīr* from 'Isma ibn Mālik ﷺ that the Prophet of Allāh ﷺ has said, "Woe unto you! When 'Umar ﷺ passes away then you should depart from this world."[67]

Now according to the detractor's ill-logic, if the general goodness of an era remains in the blessed time of the three Caliphs (*Khulafā*), nay, only in the blessed era of Sayyidunā Abū Bakr ﷺ and Sayyidunā 'Umar ﷺ (the *Shaykhayn*), then whatever is innovated thereafter becomes a blameworthy innovation by default, even if this innovation is introduced during the time of Sayyidunā 'Alī ﷺ.

---

[65] *Al-Mustadrak li al-Hākim*, the book on Ma'rifat al-Sahāba, *Amr al-Nabī* ﷺ *Li Abī Bakrin Bi Imāmat al-Nās Fī al-Salāh*, Dār al-Fikr, Beirut, v.3, p.77.
[66] *Izālat al-Khafā*, with reference to Sahl ibn Abī Hathma, Chapter Five, Suhayl Academy, Lahore, v.1, p.124.
[67] *Al-Mu'jam al-Kabīr*, Hadīth #478, al-Maktabat al-Faysiliyyah, Beirut, v.17. p.181.

Allāh forbid! May the Sublime Lord protect us from unwanted thoughts.

What is more interesting to note is that one **cannot** contrast the Hadīth about "The best of people is my century..." with these Ahādīth [Both succinctly refer to the goodness of the time without ever mentioning the excellence or evil of innovation. This is an extrapolation on the part of the critics.] Now read what has been written in *Izālat al-Khafā* by Shāh Waliullāh ad-Dehlawī ﷺ, who is the Grandfather and Grand Shaykh (*Pīr*) of the "great Imam" Ismāil ad-Dehlawī[68]. The former has given a very unique[69] interpretation to this Hadīth:

"There is another meaning to the Hadīth ('The best of people are my century...') and that is: the first period of time (*Qarn*) begins with the Prophet's migration ﷺ to Madinah the Illumined until his departure from this world. The second period of time is the beginning of the Caliphate of Sayyidunā Abū Bakr ﷺ until the demise of Sayyidunā 'Umar ﷺ. The third period starts with the Caliphate of Sayyidunā 'Uthmān ibn 'Affān ﷺ, and the duration of each period is approximately twelve years. *Qarn* literally means a group of people whose age is very similar. Then later this word was used to describe that nation whose political leadership and government (Caliphate) were similar. When the government

---

[68] Ismāil ad-Dehlawī's books such as *Taqwiyat al-Imān*, *Īdāh al-Haqq*, *al-Sirāt al-Mustaqīm*, etc. form the basis of Wahhābism in the Indo-Pakistani region. He strayed far from the Sunnī and Naqshbandī Sufi path of his illustrious forefathers (http://mac.abc.se/home/onesr/d/tqi_e.pdf).

[69] This interpretation is unique because it very narrowly defines the time of each period (*Qarn*), whilst the generally accepted timeframe established by the Hadīth is: the first three centuries in the age of the Muslim Community or the first four hundred years after the Prophet ﷺ. Shāh Waliullāh ﷺ wrote *Izālat al-Khafā* in order to address Shi'a claims concerning the nature of the Caliphate and the superiority of Sayyidunā 'Ali ﷺ.

changes together with its ministers, mayors, soldiers and other people of the government then we say the *Qarn* has changed."[70]

He writes in another place, "The first *Qarn* is the time from the migration till the demise of the Holy Prophet ﷺ, the second *Qarn* is the time of Sayyidunā Abū Bakr as-Siddīq ؓ and Sayyidunā 'Umar ؓ (the *Shaykhayn*) and the third *Qarn* is the time of 'Uthmān ibn 'Affān ؓ. Thereafter controversies and tribulations appeared."[71]

There is no doubt that the above meaning [of this quote] is also possible, thus proving that anything which was not present during the first three periods (*Qarn*) as *Bid'at* and misguidance is baseless. [Otherwise, Companions like Sayyidunā 'Alī ؓ and the majority of the Successors were not saved from such innovations, Allāh forbid, as per the detractor's dubious inference and hoax!].

POINT 7

According to the Hadīth under discussion ("The best of people are my century..."), one might conclude that anything innovated during the Prophet's century ﷺ must be good. But what about the Hadīth mentioned by Imām Tirmidhī ؓ through an excellent (*Hasan*) chain? This Hadīth is narrated by Hadrat Anas ؓ and Imām Ahmad [ibn Hanbal ؓ], who narrates from Hadrat 'Ammār ibn Yāsir ؓ. Ibn Hibbān ؓ narrates in his *Sahīh* from Hadrat 'Ammār ibn Yāsir ؓ and Salmān Fārsī ؓ. Likewise, Shaykh 'Abd al-Haqq ؓ has also authenticated this Hadīth, in which, the Prophet of Allāh ﷺ said, "The example of my Community

---

[70] *Izālat al-Khafā*, with reference to Sahl ibn Abī Hathma, chapter five, Suhayl Academy, Lahore, v.1, p.75.
[71] Ibid., p.121.

(*Ummah*) is like the rain. It is not known whether the first part is the best or the latter part."[72]

Shaykh 'Abd al-Haqq ﷽ writes in its commentary, "This Hadīth refers to the whole *Ummah* being the best like rain in that every part is beneficial."[73]

Imām Muslim ﷽ narrates in his *Sahīh* that the Messenger of Allāh ﷺ said, "There shall always remain a group from my *Ummah* who will stay firm on the command of Allāh, anyone who leaves them or goes against them shall not harm them (as they will remain in this state of submission) until the promise of Allāh is fulfilled, and they will be dominant over the people."[74]

Shāh Waliullāh ﷽ writes in his *Izālat al-Khafā*, "Don't believe for a second that all of the people of the evil times are evil, or that the blessings of Allāh will prove ineffective in cleansing their souls. Actually there is a very startling secret contained in the poet's verse:

You have mentioned all the defects of wine, but mention its goodness!
To keep the layman's heart, don't totally disregard its goodness!

The divine power (*Qudrat*) of Allāh has always produced a group of people who become centres of Light and Blessings."[75]

Now where have the specifications [that narrowly define] the earlier Hadīth ("The best of people are my century...") gone?

---

[72] *Jāmi' al-Tirmidhī*, the chapter on *al-Amthāl*, Amīn Company, Delhi, v.2, p.110
Musnad Ahmad ibn Hanbal, narrated from Anas ﷽, Beirut, v.3, p.143.
[73] *Ashi'at al-Lam'āt*, the chapter on al-Manākib wa al-Fadāil, chapter on *Thawāb Hādhihi al-Ummah*, Hadīth#4228, Nūriya Razawiyya, Sikhar, v.4, p.753.
[74] *Sahīh al-Muslim*, Kitāb al-Amārāt, Qadīmī Kutub Khāna, Karachi, v.2, p.143.
[75] *Izālat al-Khafā*, chapter five, Suhayl Academy, Lahore, v.1, p.145.

And why shouldn't the practices of the Sufi saints be classified as good, even though they were introduced later on? [It was the wont of the opponents to misuse such texts to support their new-fangled theories, especially when attacking "suspect practices" (better known as praiseworthy innovations) and "Sufi excess." But Shāh Waliullāh ﷺ did not harbour these mistaken notions, nor did he deny the existence of goodness amongst the latter-day Muslims (*Khalaf*).]

POINT 8

If we reflect upon the reports of the Companions it clarifies one point that even in their statements they did not regard a thing as good or evil due to the time. There are innumerable things that were innovated after the blessed time of the Beloved Prophet ﷺ that the Companions rebuked and condemned. On the other hand, they also praised and acted upon other innovations.

Amīr al-Mu'minīn ʿUmar ibn al-Khattāb ﷺ has said as regards to the Tarāwīh prayer with Jama'at, "How good is this innovation (*Bid'ah*)."[76]

Sayyidunā 'Abdullāh ibn 'Umar ﷺ said regarding the early morning prayers (*Duhā*), "Indeed it is an innovation and how good it is. It is amongst the best things people have innovated."[77]

Sayyidunā Abū Amāma al-Bāhilī ﷺ states, "You have innovated standing during the month of Ramadān. Thus you should keep practising it and never neglect it."[78]

---

[76] *Sahīh al-Bukhārī*, the book of *al-Sawm*, the chapter on *Man Qāma Ramadāna*, Qadīmī Kutub Khāna, Karachi, v.1, p.269.
[77] *Al-Mu'jam al-Kabīr*, Hadiīth#13563, Al-Maktabat al-Faisaliyya, Beirut, v.12, p.424.

These Companions regarded some innovations as good. Yet when Sayyidunā 'Abdullāh ibn 'Umar ⬧ heard someone give the reminder-call to prayer (*Tathwīb*), he said: "Let us get away from this innovator (*Mubtadi*)."[79]

Similarly, when Sayyidunā 'Abdullāh ibn al-Mughaffal ⬧ heard his son recite *Bismillāh* loudly in his prayers, he replied, "O son! Stay away from these new (innovated) things."[80]

These actions occurred during the lifetime of the blessed Companions; nevertheless, they still regarded some of these deeds as blameworthy innovations. Thus, we see that the Companions gave us a clear criterion by which to judge, not as per their century, but rather as per the act itself. If they saw no contradiction to the *Shari'ah*, then they would allow it. But if they sensed even the slightest contradiction to the Sacred Law, then they would forbid it. This was the same procedure during the time of the Successors (*Tābi'īn*) and thereafter.

The Companions would approve of certain innovations and disapprove of other innovations. Surely, they must have had a standard by which to judge, and each deed was judged according to the goodness or wickedness of the act itself. Thus all the Companions, their Successors (*Tābi'īn*) and the Successors of the Successors (*Taba' Tābi'īn*) agreed that goodness will always remain good though it may be new, and evil will always remain evil even if it is old. By the Grace of Allāh Almighty, our law is the Divine

---

[78] *Al-Mu'jam al-Awsat*, Hadīth#7446, v.8, p.218.
al-Durr al-Manthur, under the verse 57:27, v.8. p.64.
[79] *Al-Musannaf Li 'Abd al-Razzāq*, the chapter of *at-Tathwīb Fī al-Adhān wa al-Iqāmah*, al-Maktab al-Islāmī, Beirut, v.1, p.475.
[80] *Jāmi' al-Tirmidhī*, the book on al-Salāh, the chapter on *Ma Jā'a Fi Tark al-Hajr*, *Āmīn* company, Delhi vol. 1, p.33.

Law which shall remain so till the Day of Judgment; it is not a man-made law that will change every so often.

POINT 9

The objection that "Our great predecessors have not acted upon it so how can we?" has been answered already in the previous point. Here we shall present the statements of our liege-lords, Sayyidunā Abū Bakr as-Siddīq ❖ and Sayyidunā 'Umar ❖, to prove that the action itself must be praiseworthy for it to be acted upon, even though our predecessors may not have done so.

It is in *al-Bukhārī* narrated by Zayd ibn Thābit ❖: Abū Bakr as-Siddīq ❖ sent for me when the Muslims of Yamāma had been killed[81]. I went to him and found 'Umar ibn al-Khattāb ❖ sitting with him. Abū Bakr ❖ then said: "'Umar ❖ has come to me and said, 'Casualties were heavy among the Qur'ān reciters (*Qurra'*) on the day of the Battle of Yamāma. I am afraid that more heavy casualties may take place among the Qur'ān reciters (*Qurra'*) on other battlefields, whereby a large part of the Qur'ān may be lost. Therefore I suggest that you order that the Qur'ān be collected.'" I said to 'Umar: "How can you do something which Allāh's Prophet ❀ did not do?" 'Umar ❖ replied: "By Allāh, this is a praiseworthy project."

'Umar ❖ kept on urging me to accept his proposal until Allāh opened up my breast to that and I began to realize the inherent goodness in the idea. Then Abū Bakr ❖ said to me, "You are a wise young man and we have no suspicion about you, and you

---

[81] These Companions were martyred when they fought against the false prophet, Musaylama the Liar, in the Battle of Yamāma.

used to write the Revelation for Allāh's Prophet ﷺ so you should search for (the fragmentary scripts of) the Qur'ān[82] and collect it."

Zayd ibn Thābit ؓ then states, "By Allāh, if they had ordered me to move one of the mountains that would not have been a weightier task for me than ordering me to collect the Qur'ān. Then I said to Abū Bakr ؓ, "How will you do something which Allāh's Messenger ﷺ did not do?" Abū Bakr ؓ replied, "By Allāh, it is better." Abū Bakr kept on urging me to accept 'Umar's idea until Allāh expanded my breast and made me incline to that which He opened the breasts of Abū Bakr and 'Umar to."[83]

The upshot of this Hadīth is that Zayd ibn Thābit ؓ expressed his concern to two of the greatest Companions, Sayyidunā Abū Bakr as-Siddīq ؓ and Sayyidunā 'Umar ؓ, about doing something that the Messenger of Allāh ﷺ did not do. They did not reply by saying, "We are in the best of all times so it is permissible to innovate this," but rather they said, "If it is better than leaving it off then we should implement it." And upon this reply the Holy Qur'ān was collated by the agreement of the Companions. Now is it really surprising that the deviant sects criticise things which have already been solved by the Companions?

---

[82] When the Holy Qu'ran was being reveled the Companions used to inscribe it on whatever they had on hand such as palm stalks and thin white stones. They also preserved it in their breasts through constant recitation. As the reader may already know, the Qu'rān was disclosed to our Master Prophet Muhammad ﷺ over a period of 23 years. Zaid ibn Thābit ؓ was entrusted with the awesome responsibility of collecting all these fragmentary scripts to ensure that *every* verse of the Holy Qu'rān was safely preserved.

[83] *Sahīh al-Bukhārī*, the book on *Fadāil al-Qur'ān* the chapter on *Jama' al-Qur'ān*, Qadīmī Kutub Khāna, Karachi, v.2, p.745.

POINT 10

The objection made against us [that we engage in religious actions that were not present at the time of the Pious Predecessors (*Salaf*)] can be made to the Successors of the Successors (*Taba' Tābi'īn*) in respect to the Successors (*Tābi'īn*), and to the Successors (*Tābi'īn*) in respect to the Companions, and to the Companions in respect to the Prophet of Allāh ﷺ.

For example, the critics do not call anything that was innovated during the time of the Successors of the Successors (*Taba' Tābi'īn*) innovation (*Bid'ah*). Although the objection could be made that if that innovation was good then the Successors (*Tābi'īn*), Companions and the Prophet ﷺ should have implemented it. Are the Successors of the Successors (*Taba' Tābi'īn*) more concerned about their Religion (*Dīn*) than their predecessors? Similarly, the same thing can be said about the Successors (*Tābi'īn*) in contrast to the Companions and so forth. Anything the Companions innovated or agreed upon in terms of its goodness as an innovation can be objected too!

Did the Prophet of Allāh ﷺ not know about the goodness of those (good) innovations? Or were the Companions more concerned about implementing goodness than the Messenger of Allāh ﷺ? Allāh forbid! In short, the deviants have raised such baseless objections by which all the Companions and the Successors (*Tābi'īn*) will be labelled innovators, Allāh forbid!

But the rule is: "To do something is different and to forbid something is different." If the Prophet of Allāh ﷺ has not done something or he did not object to it, then who is there to forbid the Companions from acting upon it? If the Companions have not done something, then who dare forbid the Successors (*Tābi'īn*) from acting upon it? And so forth.

Isn't it puzzling that if the Prophet ﷺ and the Companions and the Successors (*Tābi'īn*) have not acted upon something, the deviants allow the Successors of the Successors (*Taba' Tābi'īn*) to act upon it? Yet if the Successors of the Successors (*Taba' Tābi'īn*) have not acted upon something, then suddenly the doors of implementation are closed for those after them! Is there any limit to their ignorance? It will be much better if they were to implement the teachings of their great Imām, Nawāb Siddīq Hasan Khān Bhopāl, who said, "Whatever the Prophet ﷺ has not done is innovation and misguidance." Whether the Companions, or the Successors (*Tābi'īn*), implement this new action, it is still a blameworthy innovation (*Bid'ah*). Thus, this ignorant chap then deemed Amīr al-Mu'minīn 'Umar ؓ as an innovator *due to* his innovation of praying the Tarāwīh prayers in congregation and made the abhorred soul of their spiritual guide, 'Abdullāh ibn Sabā very happy. May Allāh protect us [from such corruption]!

POINT 11

Imām 'Allāma Ahmad ibn Muhammad al-Qastalānī ؒ a commentator of *Sahīh al-Bukhārī* writes in *Mawāhib al-Laduniyya*, "The permissibility can be deduced by the act itself, but the impermissibility of the act cannot be deduced by not acting upon it."

Shāh 'Abd al-'Azīz ad-Dehlawī ؒ writes in *Tuhfā Ithnā 'Ashariyya*, "Something may not be acted upon, but this is not the same thing as prohibiting it."[84]

---

[84] *Tuhfā Ithnā 'Ashariyya*, chapter ten, Suhayl Academy, Lahore, p.269.

This is the deviants' ignorance that they prohibit things that have not been prohibited!

POINT 12

The reality is that the Companions and the Successors (*Tābi'īn*) did not have time for this desirable (*Mustahab*) act. They were engaged in spreading the word of Islām, protecting the religion, fighting against the rebels, rectifying the Islāmic state, extinguishing the fire of misguidance, widening the Divine Law, defending faith (*Imān*) and so forth. Let alone this they did not even have the opportunity to establish the rules and regulations about the fundamentals (*Usūl*) and their particulars, to compose, compile and to write books of knowledge and evidences to answer the objections of the innovators. Nevertheless, when by the Grace of Allāh, the roots of the tree of Islām became firm in the west and in the east, the true savants and scholars of the Religion (*Dīn*), relying upon the Mercy of the True Gardener (Allāh Almighty), began to occupy themselves with important tasks at that time without fearing the arrival of dust storms and hot winds. Thereafter we see light rainfall and the correct minds ploughed into the ground of research until we see pure research flowing. The eyes of the scholars and the Sufi saints (*Awliyā*) watered the garden, the pure winds of their piety bought freshness, and we finally see the garden of the Chosen One (*Mustafā*) 🌸 coming into full bloom. The flowers and the flora leave the eye, mouth, and mind bewildered. All praise belongs to Allāh!

Now if an ignorant person objects by saying, "Where were these flowers before? Where were these branches? These are all new. If there was any goodness in them then why did the people in the past not cultivate them?" To answer his stupidity a flower from the Divine garden would laugh out and say, "O ignoramus! The people of the past were occupied with planting the seeds of this garden so that they might take root. If they were alive today, then assuredly they would have been delighted with all of this!" But the objector will be deprived from such delight as a result of his stupidity.

Now the reader will understand this parable, a fire broke out in a wise man's house. His children, expensive furniture, and wealth are trapped inside. The wise man did not pay any attention to the furniture or wealth, but risking his life, he went into the house to save his children. Then a fire broke out in a simpleton's house. He has no children, but a lot of wealth. He stood there staring at his house. Onlookers asked him to go inside and take some of his wealth out before the house burnt down. He answers saying, "Are you daft? That wise man left his wealth inside his house; I should imitate him and leave my wealth inside too!" This ignorant person did not understand the fact that the wise man had a more important duty, and that was to protect his children. He did not leave his wealth behind merely imagining it to be worthless!

POINT 13

Let us assume that anything that was not present in the best of times is forbidden. Then the detractors should look no further than their own veranda, because the establishment of Islāmic schools, and the practice of asking for donations, buying discounted books, fixing the day for giving speeches to Friday, financing such events, attending banquets, organizing debates that are presided by judges, writing refutations and publishing them, undertaking missionary trips from city to city, attaining a certificate of mastery in the science of Hadīth after studying each Hadīth book and thousands of other things, which are commonplace today amongst their scholars and the general public, did not exist in the best of times. Can they cite even one example of such actions being practiced during the first three centuries of Islām?

What else can we say about the elite of this new trend? Those who take money in exchange of stamping verdicts, who have the verdicts of both the claimant and the defendant [ready at hand waiting for a bribe from the highest bidder]. If they go for *Hajj* they have a receipt of commission from Mumbai and Delhi! Perhaps these things were present during the best of times or maybe they have received a Divine mandate that gives them permission to do whatever they want. Or maybe these criticisms are only made when it relates to the dignity and honour of the Beloved Prophet of Allāh ﷺ and the rest is permissible and unaccountable! There is no power or might except from Allāh.

POINT 14

What a pity! The times have changed in relation to the respect and honour [that the rank and file among the Muslims would show to the Messenger of Allāh ﷺ]. The scholars never thought to take into account all the specific mannerisms mentioned in the Ahādīth, because from the very beginning to the present day, traditional etiquette (*Adab*) followed one rule, "Any mannerism which is more virtuous in terms of honouring the dignity of the Prophet of Allāh ﷺ is good" (as mentioned by the great Imām Sayyidunā Kamāl al-Millah wad-Dīn Muhammad ﷺ in *Fath al-Qadīr*[85] and elaborated by his student Shaykh Rahmatullah Sindhī ﷺ in *al-Mansak al-Mutawassit*, which was approved by Mawlānā Mullā 'Alī al-Qārī ﷺ in *al-Maslak al-Mutaqassit*. This has also been the preferred view in *'Ālamgirī* etc.).

---

[85] *Fath al-Qadīr*, the book on al-Hajj, Masāil Manthūra, Makba'e Nūriya Razawiyya, Sikhar, v.3, p.94.

We have already mentioned the statement of Imām Ibn Hajar ﷺ (in point two), "All modes of respect for the Prophet of Allāh ﷺ, which are free from associating partnership with Allāh, are recommended according to those whose insight has been illuminated by Allāh Almighty."

Therefore from the past until the present, if Muslims innovated a new way of honouring the Prophet of Allāh ﷺ then the scholars have praised and not (Allāh forbid) condemned it by calling it innovation (*Bid'ah*) and misguidance. This calamity is only widespread among those deviants that ask without fail, "When did so and so do this?" Although they do thousands of things which so and so did not do! This is all to degrade the honour of the Prophet of Allāh ﷺ and we should keep answering them by saying:

بعد از خدا بزرگ تونی قصہ مختصر

In short, after Allāh, the most honourable person is you ﷺ

Speak as much as possible anytime and anywhere about loving and honouring the Beloved of Allāh ﷺ. In the end, their Imām [Ismāil ad-Dihlawī] has already clarified in *Taqwiyat al-Imān* [Strengthening the Faith[86]] that one should respect the Prophet of Allāh ﷺ as an older brother, or even less than that. This is their religion, this is their faith and this is their claim. (That is why their official creedal statement, *Taqwiyat al-Imān*, should be titled *Tafwiyat al-Imān* [Weakening the Faith]). There is no power or might except from Allāh!

In any case, the discussion will go on. If I was to collate the new ways that were introduced in honouring the Beloved of Allāh ﷺ

---

[86] *Taqwiyat al-Imān*, chapter five, Matba' 'Alīmī, Andron Lohari gate, Lahore, p.42.

and which has been practised by the great scholars then a whole book can be compiled. Nevertheless, I will suffice by mentioning a few examples.

EXAMPLE 1

Sayyidunā Imām Mālik ﷺ, the scholar of Madinah the Illumined, introduced new etiquette (*Adab*) when narrating the Aḥādīth. His particular mannerisms cannot be traced back to the era of the Companions, nor the Successors (*Tabi'īn*). Yet the scholars have regarded such acts as an expression of his ardent love and respect for the Beloved of Allāh ﷺ. Imām al-Qādī 'Iyād ﷺ writes in his renowned book *al-Shifā*:

Hadrat Muttarraf ﷺ narrates that whenever people would approach Imām Mālik ﷺ, he would inform his servant to ask them if they came to inquire about a Hadīth or an Islāmic ruling. If they wanted to know about the latter then the Imām would come out of his room and answer their questions.

If they came to know about the former, then he would bathe, wear clean clothes, a green shawl, and tie a turban. He would then put on some scent. A special chair would be placed on which he would sit and then he would narrate the Hadīth with sincere humbleness. Incense would be left to burn as long as he remained seated. When he was asked about all this, he answered, "I like to respect the Aḥādīth of the Messenger of Allāh ﷺ in this manner."[87]

---

[87] *Al-Shifā Bi Ta'rīf Huqūq al-Mustafā* ﷺ, chapter two, al-Matba' al-Sharikat al-Sahhāfiyya, v.2, pp.38-39.

EXAMPLE 2

Imām Mālik ﷺ would never ride on any type of transportation in the blessed city of Madinah the Illumined. He would say, "I feel ashamed in front of Allāh, how can I ride on an animal that will trod the ground in which my Beloved ﷺ is resting."[88]

EXAMPLE 3

Imām Abū 'Abd ar-Rahmān ﷺ mentions that Imām Ahmad ibn al-Fadlawiyy al-Zāhid ﷺ would never hold a bow without *Wudū* after he heard that the Messenger of Allāh ﷺ also held a bow in his blessed hand.[89]

EXAMPLE 4

Imām Ibn Hāj al-Mālikī ﷺ, who is a reliable source in the eyes of the opponents and who was extreme in condemning innovations, writes in *al-Mudkhal*, "There were certain pious predecessors who stayed within the vicinity of the Haram of Makkah yet they would never relieve themselves in the Haram, nor did they lie down. (I say) for such people it is desirable (*Mustahab*) for them to stay in the vicinity of the Haram, rather they should be ordered to stay."[90]

EXAMPLE 5

It is in the same book, "There were some who would come to pay a visit to the Prophet of Allāh ﷺ in Madinah. They would not even enter the blessed city, but instead they would pay their respect

---

[88] Ibid., v.2, p.48.
[89] Ibid.
[90] *Al-Mudkhal*, the chapter on *Dhikr Ba'ad Mā Ya'tūru al'Hājj Fī Hajjihi*, Dāal al-Kitāb al-'Arabī, v.4, p.253.

from outside. They were asked about this so they replied, 'How can we enter the blessed city of the Beloved of Allāh 🌸? We do not regard ourselves as worthy of entering this sacred vicinity.'"[91]

EXAMPLE 6

Quoting again from the same book, "My teacher (Imām Abū Muhammad 🌸) states, 'As long as I remained in the Masjid of the Beloved 🌸, I never sat down except in prayers. I remained in standing position until our convoy left.'"[92]

EXAMPLE 7

Imām Ibn Hāj al-Mālikī 🌸 transmits the following anecdote about the same Shaykh, "I (Imām Abū Muhammad 🌸) never went to Baqī' leaving the presence of the Beloved 🌸 nor have I paid respects to anyone else besides the Beloved Prophet 🌸. Once I thought of going to Baqī' then I asked myself: 'Where shall you go? Here is the Door of Allāh open for the beggars, the deprived, and for the unfortunate and regretful people. And who else is there (in Baqī') besides the Prophet of Allāh 🌸 whom we shall visit? Whoever acts upon this will gain success and his desires will be fulfilled.'"[93]

Now this beggar of Sayyidunā ash-Shaykh Muhyid'dīn 'Abd al-Qādir al-Jīlānī 🌸 completes this verdict with the same words, whosoever acts upon this [standing (*Qiyām*) during the *Mawlid*] will gain success and his desires will be fulfilled, Allāh Willing.

---

[91] Ibid., the chapter in al-Kalām 'Alā Ziyārat Sayyid al-Awwalīn wa al-Ākhirīn,v.1, p.254.
[92] Ibid., v.1, p.259.
[93] Ibid., v.1, p.259.

And I hope, by the Grace of Allāh, that this *Fatwā* not only becomes useful in understanding the ruling about standing (*Qiyām*), but that it also provides meaningful insights into many contradictory issues and is a means to guidance for those whom Allāh wills.

There is no power or might except from Allāh Almighty. And peace and blessing be upon the best of His creation, the sun of His universe, our master and patron Muhammad 🕌 and upon his Family and all of the Companions. Āmīn! Āmīn! Āmīn!

- Imām Ahmad Ridā Khān ⚜
(`Abd al-Mustafā 🕌)

Endorsements

This verdict has been endorsed and stamped by the following scholars:

1. Hadrat Muhammad Gowhar 'Alī ﷺ
2. Hadrat 'Abdullāh ﷺ
3. Hadrat Muhammad Irshād Husayn Ahmadī ﷺ
4. Hadrat Muhammad 'Abd al-Qādir Muhibb-e-Rasūl Qādirī ﷺ
5. Hadrat Imdād Husayn ﷺ
6. Hadrat Hāfidh Bakhsh Muhammad ﷺ
7. Hadrat 'Abd al-Muqtadir al-`Uthmānī al-Qādirī ﷺ
8. Hadrat 'Abd al-Razzāq ibn 'Abd al-Samad ﷺ
9. Hadrat Muhammad Salāmat Allāh Abū al-Dhakā Sirāj al-Dīn ﷺ
10. Hadrat Muhammad Shāh ﷺ
11. Hadrat Sultān Ahmad ﷺ

Their comments can be viewed from the original Urdu *Fatwā* published in *Fatāwā-e-Radawiyya* [The Legal Edicts of Imām Ahmad Ridā], Raza Foundation, Lahore v.26, p. 550-552.

This translation was completed on Monday, May 1st 2011 CE, which corresponds to the 25th of Jumad al-Ukhra 1432 AH.

Concerning the Author

Shaykh al-Islām Imām Ahmad Ridā Khān al-Qādirī ؓ was born in 1856 CE in the western United Provinces of British India just a year before the great Indian Revolt. His ancestors were Pathāns, valiant and high-minded warriors, who probably migrated from Qandahar (in present-day Afghanistan) in the seventieth century. His grandfather, Mawlānā Ridā 'Alī Khān ؓ (d. 1866), made a break from soldiering to become a scholar and Sufi. This noble tradition was carried on by his son, Mawlānā Naqī 'Alī Khān ؓ (d. 1880), under whom Imām Ahmad Ridā Khān ؓ completed the Dars-e-Nizami syllabus studying a range of twenty-one Islāmic sciences by the age of thirteen. Both father and son were disciples (*Murids*) of Sayyid Al-e Rasūl ؓ (d. 1879) of Marehra, a descendent of the Prophet ﷺ through his daughter Sayyida Fatima ؓ and a Sufi saint par excellence.

In 1878 and again in 1905, Imām Ahmad Ridā Khān ؓ undertook the pilgrimage to Makkah the Ennobled. On both occasions he received recognition from top-ranking scholars. Several of his works were commended such as:

- *Fatāwā al-Haramayn bi Rajf Nadwat al-Mayn* [Edicts of the Sacred Sanctuaries shaking the lying council], which was published in 1900 and endorsed by sixteen scholars from Makkah;
- *Kifl al-Faqih al-Fahim fi Ahkam Qirtas al-Darahim* [Guarantee of the Discerning Jurist on Duties relating to Paper

70

Money], a celebrated work that was penned and praised during his second Hajj;

- *Husām al-Haramayn* [The Sword of the Sacred Sanctuaries], which was certified by twenty scholars from Makkah and thirteen from Madinah, these luminaries belonged to the Hanafī, Shāfiʿī and Mālikī schools of Islāmic jurisprudence;
- *Al-Dawlah al-Makkiyyah biʾl Maddat al-Ghaybiyya* [The Makkan Realm on the Matter of the Unseen], which is a definitive masterpiece on the Prophet's knowledge of the unseen 舙. This monograph has received seventy-seven endorsements from the scholars of Hijaz, Yemen, Syria and Egypt.

Imām Ahmad Ridā Khān 舙 is best known for three areas of research: (1) defending the honour of the Master of the Messengers 舙, (2) attacking blameworthy innovators who disguised themselves as Sunnis and Sufis, and (3) delivering formal legal edicts (*Fatāwā*) according to the clear and popular Hanafī legal school. Due to his indefatigable service to Islām, encyclopedic knowledge and spiritual prowess (*Taqwā*)[94], venerable scholars and muftis from the Arab world and his native India declared him to be a Renewer (*Mujaddid*) of the fourteenth Islāmic Hijri. Even contemporary *'Ulamā* like Shaykh Sayyid Muhammad Abul Hudā al-Yaqoubi of Syria, may Allāh increase his stature, have acknowledged that, in the Subcontinent, Imām Ahmad Ridā Khān 舙 is among the most famous of all scholars in modern times and a *Mujaddid*[95].

---

[94] *Taqwā*: God-wariness, one of the most highly praised human qualities in the Holy Qurʾān, which is closely connected to *Ihsān*, perfection of belief and practice.

[95] A transcript from the *Takbeer TV* interview with Shaykh Sayyid Muhammad Abul Hudā al-Yaqoubi (accessed on July 23, 2011) is available at

One of Imām Ahmad Ridā Khān's greatest contributions to Islāmic literature is without doubt, *Kanz al-Imān* [A Treasury of Faith], which is reputed to be the Holy Qur'ān in the Urdu language. Likewise his Arabic, Persian and Urdu poetry is inspiring and beautiful, especially *Mustafā Jān e Rahmat* [Mustafā 🌺 the Paragon of Mercy]. This poem in praise of the Chosen One 🌺 is traditionally recited during religious celebrations such as the *Mawlid*, not only in the Subcontinent, but also in other parts of the world. Those who have read his *Al-Malfūz al-Sharīf* [Utterances] will testify to his deep and abiding love for the Sufi saints (*Awliyā*), and the 'Ulamā of the *Ahl al-Sunnah wa al-Jamā'ah*. He also wrote a significant tract against desecrating mausoleums[96], which should be in the home of very Sunni Muslim and on the shelves of traditional, mainstream Islamic institutes. It admonishes Muslims to follow the Sunnah of our Master Prophet Muhammad 🌺 and forsake the extremism of the Wahhābi/"Salafi" sect.

Imām Ahmad Ridā Khān 🌺 left this mundane world on Friday, the 25th of Safar, 1340 AH (October 28, 1921). It was the exact time of the Jumu'ah Adhān. His blessed mausoleum in the town of Bareilly, India is still a place of pious visitation for scholars and laymen alike.

May Allāh, the Sublime and Exalted, keep us steadfast on the way (*Maslak*) of Shaykh al-Islām Imām Ahmad Ridā Khān al-Qādirī 🌺, Āmīn.

---

http://www.sunniport.com/books/transcript%20shaykh%20yaqubi%20on%20ala hazrat.pdf.

[96] *Ihlāk ul Wahābiyyīn ala Tawhīn Qubūr il Muslimīn* [Respect for the Graves of Muslims]

Glossary

Abjad: the science of numerology.

Adab: traditional etiquette.

Ahl al-Sunnah wa al-Jamā'ah: the Sunnis; the People of the Prophetic Way and the Majority of Scholars.

Amīr al-Mu'minīn: Commander of the Faithful, a title usually reserved for the Rightly-Guided Caliphs.

Aqida, pl. *Aqaid:* doctrine.

Awliyā: the Sufi saints.

Bid'ah: innovation.

Bid'ah Hasanah: a good innovation.

Bid'ah Sayyi'ah: blameworthy innovation

Dīn: the Religion of Islām, a set of teachings, including *Tawhid* (or the affirmation of Divine Oneness) and submission to Allāh, that Allāh perfected for Prophet Muhammad ﷺ and his followers.

Dhikr: the remembrance of Allāh.

Duhā: supererogatory mid-morning prayer.

Faqih, pl. *Fuqahā*: scholar of *fiqh* or jurisprudence; generally, a person of knowledge.

Fiqh: jurisprudence.

Fatwā, pl. *Fatāwā*: a legal edict.

Ghayr Muqallidīn: those who do not follow one of the four schools of Islāmic jurisprudence.

Hafidh: one whose knowledge encompasses at least 100,000 Ahādīth in both their texts and chains of transmission.

Hajj: pilgrimage.

Halāl: lawful, permissible.

Harām: unlawful, prohibited.

Haramayn: the Makkan and Madinan Sanctuaries.

Harra: The Battle of Harra was fought at Harra, a city lying northeast of Madinah the Illumined, in 61 AH. Abdullāh ibn Zubayr ♦ and several notable Companions from Madinah fought against the Umayyad army after news of Imām Husain's ♦ martyrdom (*Shahāda*) reached them. It was the second most infamous battle during the reign of Yazid as his soldiers brought death and destruction to the people of Madinah and even attacked the Holy Kāb'a in Makkah the Ennobled.

Hasan: good, excellent or desirable (applied to the chain of transmission of a Hadīth).

Hayy: the Ever-Living.

Hujjat: legislative evidence; proof.

Hujjat al-Islām: Proof of Islām, a title reserved for exemplary Islāmic scholars, like Imām al-Ghazzālī ♦. These men of Allāh are a living example of the message and manifest proof.

Ihsān: perfection of belief and practice.

Ijmā': consensus of the scholars.

Ijtihad: personal effort of qualified legal reasoning.

Ikhtilāf al-Ummah: difference of opinion.

Imān: faith.

Juz`iyyah*, pl. *Juz`iyyāt: a specific legal injunction.

Karbalā: the Battle of Karbalā took place on the 10th of Muharram in the year 61 AH. Sayyidunā Imām Husain ibn 'Alī ♦ opposed the Caliphate of Yazid, who came to power after the death of his

74

father, Sayyidunā Muāwiyah ﷺ. Yazid was a corrupt reprobate, unfit to rule so Imām Husain ﷺ set out for Kufa with his family and friends to gather support. The Umayyad army forced them to camp at Karbalā, and a battle ensued. Allāh the Exalted chose martyrdom (*Shahāda*) for Imām Husain ﷺ on that fateful day.

Khalaf: the Followers, i.e. all Muslims who lived after the first three centuries.

Khawārij: "Outsiders," a sect who considered all Muslims who did not follow them, disbelievers. The great Hanafī scholar, 'Allāma Muhammad ibn 'Alī al-Shāmī ﷺ, applied the name of *Khawārij* to the Wahhābi movement in his celebrated *Rad al-Muhtār ala al-Dur al-Mukhtār* [Answer to the Perplexed: A Commentary on 'The Pearl']⁹⁷.

Khutba: sermon.

Kufr: unbelief.

Maddāh: a religious singer.

Madrasah: an Islāmic school.

Makrūh: disliked.

Mamnu'āt: prohibitions.

Mandūb: recommended.

Maqām al-Mahmūd: the Station of Praise.

Mawlid: commemorating the Prophet's birthday ﷺ.

Mubāh: permissible; a morally neutral action.

Mubtadi: innovator.

Muhaddith: Hadīth scholar.

Mujaddid: a Renewer (or Reviver) of the Religion. The Prophet ﷺ said: "Surely, Allāh will send for this *Ummah* at the advent of every one hundred years a person (or persons) who will renew its religion for it" (*Sunan Abū Dawūd*).

---

⁹⁷ Shaykh Muhammad Hisham Kabbani, *Encyclopedia of Islāmic Doctrine: Beliefs* (Mountain View: As-Sunna Foundation of America, 1998), 1:204.

Mujtahid, pl. *Mujtahidīn*: one who practices *ijtihad* or personal effort of qualified legal reasoning.

Muqallidīn: those who follow one of the four schools of Islāmic jurisprudence.

Mushrik: polytheist.

Mustahab: desirable.

Mustahsan: desirable, or commendable.

Mu'tazilites: "Separatists," a sect that formed in the third century and adhered to a rationalist heresy.

Nawāsib: those who hate the household of the Prophet 鸞.

Pīr: a spiritual guide on the Sufi path. As Mawlānā Jalāl ad-Dīn Rūmī 鸞 noted in the *Masnavi*, *Pīrs* are the touchstone of truth.

Qādī al-Qudāt: Chief Judge.

Qarn: period of time.

Qayyūm: the Ever-Lasting.

Qiyām: standing.

Qudrat: divine power.

Qurra': Qur'ān reciters.

Rawāfid: "the Deserters or Rebels" were so called because of their rejection (*Rafd*) of the majority of the Companions, and their refusal to accept the Imāmate of Abū Bakr 鸞 and 'Umar 鸞. They are Shī'ites that split into no fewer than fourteen sub-sects.[98]

Sāhibayn: Imām Abū Hanīfa's 鸞 two closest students, Imām Abu Yūsuf Ya'qūb ibn Ibrāhīm al-Ansārī 鸞 and Imām Abū 'Abdallāh Muhammad ibn al-Hasan al-Shaybānī 鸞.

---

[98] Shaykh 'Abd al-Qādir al-Jīlānī, *Sufficient Provision for the Seekers of the Path of Truth* (Hollywood: Al-Baz Publishing, INC., 1995), tr. Muhtar Holland, 1:409.

Sahīh: sound, or healthy; a category of Hadīth whose authenticity has been proven.
Salaf: the Predecessors, i.e. Muslims of the first three centuries.
Salawāt: sending blessings and salutations upon the blessed Messenger 襲.
Shafā'at: intercession.
Shari'ah: the Sacred Law, or the name embracing the principles and application of Islāmic law.
Shaykhayn: Abū Bakr as-Siddīq 鑿 and 'Umar ibn al-Khattāb 鑿.
Shirk: polytheism.
Suhba: companionship.
Sunnah: the way of living and acting set down by the Prophet 襲; hence, the model that Muslims follow in order to lead a life that is pleasing to Allāh the Exalted. The basic source for the Sunnah is the Hadīth or sayings of the Prophet himself 襲 or of his Companions concerning his activities.

Taba' Tābi'īn: Successors of the Successors, those Muslims who did not live in the lifetime of the Companions, but met some of their Successors (*Tābi'īn*).
Tābi'īn: Successors, those Muslims who did not live during the lifetime of the Prophet 襲, but met some of his Companions.
Taqlīd: following qualified scholarship.
Taqwā: God-wariness, one of the most highly praised human qualities in the Holy Qur'ān, which is closely connected to *Ihsān*, perfection of belief and practice.
Tariqah: the Sufi path.
Tathwīb: the reminder-call to prayer.
Tūba: glad-tidings.

Ummah: community.
'Umūm: the general meaning (of a verse) that may be used to establish rulings.

Usūl: fundamentals of faith.

Wahhābi, pl. *Wahhābis*: the followers of Ibn Abd al-Wahhāb (d. 1792 CE), who came out of Najd (in the Eastern Arabian Peninsula) and attacked the two Noble Sanctuaries. According to 'Allāma 'Alī al-Shāmī ﷺ: "They (Wahhābis) claimed to follow the Hanbalī school, but their belief was such that, in their view, they alone are Muslims and everyone else is a *mushrik* (polytheist). Under this guise, they said that killing *Ahl al-Sunna* and their scholars was permissible, until Allāh the Exalted destroyed them in the year 1233 (1818 CE) at the hands of the Muslim army."[99] This deviant group and its sectarian offshoots promote a handful of dubious scholars including: Ibn Taymiyya and his student Ibn al-Qayyim, Ibn Abd al-Wahhāb and his Najdī epigones, Ismāil ad-Dehlawī and his admirers in the Subcontinent, and modern day "scholars" such as Bin Baz, Uthaymin, Albani, and their propagandists.[100]

Wajd: spiritual ecstasy.

Wājib, pl. *Wājibāt*: a necessary duty.

Walī, pl. *Awliyā*: a Sufi saint.

Walīma: banquet.

Wudū: ablution.

Zakāt: alms-tax.

---

[99] Shaykh Muhammad Hisham Kabbani, *Encyclopedia of Islāmic Doctrine: Beliefs* (Mountain View: As-Sunna Foundation of America, 1998), 1:51.
[100] Ibid., 1:5.

Index

Index

Lightning Source UK Ltd.
Milton Keynes UK
UKOW051117190412

191049UK00001B/6/P